£19.95

D1582997

MEGA-MERGER MAYHEM
Takeover Strategies, Battles and Controls

by

S. J. Gray and M. C. McDermott

P·C·P
Paul Chapman
Publishing Ltd

P.C.P. SERIES IN ACCOUNTING AND FINANCE

Consulting Editor: Michael J. Sherer

The aim of this series is to publish lively and readable textbooks for university, polytechnic and professional students, and important, up-to-date reference books for researchers, managers and practising accountants. All the authors have been commissioned because of their specialist knowledge of their subjects and their established reputations as lecturers and researchers. All the major topics in accounting and finance will be included, but the series will give special emphasis to recent developments in the subjects and to issues of continuing debate and controversy.

Copyright © 1989, S. J. Gray and M. C. McDermott

All rights reserved

First published 1989

Paul Chapman Publishing Ltd
London

British Library Cataloguing in Publication Data

Gray, S. J. (Sidney John), *1942–*
  Mega-merger mayhem: takeover strategies,
  battles & controls.
  1. Great Britain. Companies. Merger & takeovers
  I. Title McDermott, M.C. (Michael C.)
  338.8'3'0941

ISBN 1–85396–051–9

Typeset by DP Photosetting, Aylesbury, Bucks
Printed and bound by
St. Edmundsbury Press, Bury St. Edmunds

Contents

Preface

Those of you who like the drama and suspense of war novels will find this book fascinating! It is all there: the rising tension, the sudden attack, the frenzied battle, the glory of victory and the humiliation of defeat.

While the war that Sidney Gray and Michael McDermott describe is without violence, its economic, political and social implications for the industrialised world over the longer term may well turn out to be as dramatic as those typically associated with traditional warfare.

Vast pools of leveraged capital under the command of corporate war lords, in every respect as brave and cunning as their military counterparts, are thrown into takeover battles where, once a company is 'in play', the fighting will go on to the bitter end. Armies of consultants, bankers, lawyers, accountants, PR-experts and other advisers will, like modern day soldiers of fortune, serve the master that amasses the most power and pays the richest price. Regulators seek to keep the warring parties under control but are constantly frustrated by their manoeuvring and ever changing strategies.

'Mega-Merger Mayhem' is the epic of a war for corporate control through takeovers, as it is fought at the present time across the industrialised world. It is a relevant and timely book, telling the colourful story of the people, the companies and the tactics behind a global restructuring process that increasingly is capturing the attention and imagination of the ordinary citizen.

While the focus of the book is on the British takeover arena – quite appropriately as this is, by far, the most active and advanced market place for European mega-mergers – the authors have taken care to provide useful 'tours d'horizon' of parallel developments in other countries.

'Mega-Merger Mayhem' should appeal to a broad readership. Anyone who is interested in learning more about what is behind the dramatic headlines announcing yet another takeover battle will find Sidney Gray and Michael McDermott's text easy to read, entertaining and informative. I suspect that also professional dealmakers – if indeed they can spare the time to read a book between takeover battles – will find 'Mega-Merger Mayhem' worthwhile. The detailed account of takeover practice, regulation and tactics in the UK, together with a series of case examples, will prove relevant, particularly to those recently arrived in London from other financial centres, such as New York or Tokyo. Politicians and policy-makers across the world, interested in understanding more about conditions in the UK market as a possible role model for their own regulatory framework, will find the book equally informative. Needless to say, corporate executives, be it in the UK or elsewhere, may be well advised to study the battle experience accumulated in this book. One day they might find the knowledge gained of vital importance, should they end up as predators or targets in a future takeover fight. Finally, students at business schools and universities will find the material in this book up to date and instructive.

All in all, just as the renaissance warrior would look to his copy of Machiavelli's text as a source of inspiration for his conquests, so will today's dealmakers, advisors, regulators or interested observers find 'Mega-Merger Mayhem' rich in empirical insight on corporate takeover battles.

Martin Waldenström
Paris
February 1989

Series Editor's Foreword

Takeover battles have frequently made the headlines during the 1980s. They make good newspaper copy because of the enormous sums of money and the larger-than-life personalities involved. Takeover activity in the UK was particularly hectic in the period 1986–1988 and involved some of the largest and most well known companies in the country. Gray and McDermott's very topical book is a detailed and often critical study of the main mega-mergers during this period.

The first part of the book looks at the economic and regulatory context in which the recent spate of mega-mergers has taken place. The authors identify several reasons for the 1986–88 merger boom, including the emergence of aggressive entrepreneurs from Australasia, the acceptability of highly leveraged bids and the recognition that the value of many large UK companies lies primarily in their brand names. They also review the government's merger policy and the role of the Stock Exchange, the Takeover Panel and the accountancy profession in regulating merger activity and controlling the behaviour of those involved in takeover battles.

The second part of the book comprises seven very entertaining and informative descriptions of well known UK takeover battles. In some the bidder is acquired in acquiring the target company, in others the intended victim just managed to escape from the clutches of the bidder. However, the common characteristic of all these takeover battles was the very public and acrimonious way in which battle was enjoined and conducted. Each chapter describes the objectives and financial profile of the bidding company and its prey and provides a blow by blow description of the initial and revised bids, the tactics, the public, the secret and the somewhat dirty, employed by either side and the final outcome of the battle. The authors also use each takeover story to draw out some lessons for merger policy in the UK and to provide evidence of the difficulties faced by the regulators in controlling the behaviour of the combatants during takeover battles.

Gray and McDermott accept that the government's merger policy has been consistently applied but they argue that it tends to encourage cross-national conglomerate-type mergers at the expense of horizontal, industry-based mergers. The authors also argue strongly for all shareholders in takeover battles to be given more reliable information and they urge the accountancy profession to take the lead in recommending increased disclosure in documents used in takeover battles.

Mega-Merger Mayhem will find a place on the bookshelves of all those interested in the ownership and control of the major UK companies and the effect of merger activity on the shape of the industrial structure of the UK as it prepares for 1992 and the single European market. It is with very great pleasure, therefore, that I welcome this highly readable and informative book on mega-mergers to the Paul Chapman Accounting and Finance Series.

Michael Sherer

PART I

THE TAKEOVER ENVIRONMENT

1

Mergers and Takeovers: The Players and the Game

INTRODUCTION

This book reviews the recent merger boom in the United Kingdom, highlights the key events and discusses the major issues. It identifies the strengths and weaknesses of the Government's merger policy in action and its controls governing competition. It also examines the conduct of the combatants and the other participants in takeover battles, with particular reference to controversial mega-bids involving some of Britain's major companies. Finally, it assesses the policy implications of recent developments and puts forward some proposals for change.

The book begins with a review and assessment of the extent and nature of merger activity in the UK. For the purposes of this book the terms 'takeover', 'acquisition' and 'merger' are used synonymously, consistent with common usage, to describe business combinations irrespective of form. In order to put the UK scene in context, there is a comparative review of developments in other major industrial nations, including Japan and the USA.

The UK regulatory environment is then examined by focusing on regulatory controls at two levels: first, at the governmental merger policy level, i.e. whether or not mergers should be permitted; and second, at the corporate conduct level during the takeover process itself. As regards the former, the roles, policy and effectiveness of the Office of Fair Trading (OFT), the Monopolies and Mergers Commission (MMC) and the Secretary of State for Trade and Industry are examined. Corporate conduct, on the other hand, is policed by the City Panel on Takeovers and Mergers and by the Stock Exchange. Accounting and disclosure standards relating to takeovers and mergers are then evaluated, with particular reference to the suggestion that the existing *laissez-faire* accounting atmosphere has contributed to the merger boom by providing the flexibility for questionable, 'creative' accounting practices.

Before providing case studies of some recent takeover battles, the review of the mergers scene is continued by identifying the roles and behaviour of the advisers involved in the takeover teams, including the merchant bankers, advertising agencies, public relations consultants, accountants, solicitors and stockbrokers.

Seven case studies of billion pound-plus contested takeover bids in the UK are then examined with a view to highlighting the major issues involved, the application of merger policy in practice and the lessons to be learned. The takeover battles are examined in chronological order and comprise: Elders IXL versus Allied-Lyons, Hanson Trust versus United Biscuits for Imperial, Guinness versus Argyll for Distillers, GEC versus Plessey, Dixons versus Woolworth, BTR versus Pilkington, and Nestlé versus Jacobs Suchard for Rowntree. The cases have been selected on the basis of size, controversy and representativeness of the issues involved in mega-merger battles.

Finally, conclusions are drawn together and some lessons indicated for consideration by policy-makers and participants in the context of UK takeovers and mergers. In arriving at these views a wide variety of sources of information have been used including interviews with key participants, and archival data such as government papers and reports, corporate literature including annual reports and takeover documents, press reports, books and journal articles.

The book begins with a résumé of the major developments in merger activity in the UK. Current UK activity is compared with past trends. By so doing one can identify whether the UK is in fact undergoing a 'merger boom' in terms of the number and value of firms acquired. This chapter concludes with a brief review of merger activity in Continental Europe, Australasia, Japan and the USA.

THE UNITED KINGDOM

The changing merger scene

By 1986 the nature of target companies in the UK had been transformed. Whereas in the 1960s and 1970s the largest companies were virtually takeover-proof simply because of their size, by the mid-1980s size was no longer a deterrent against a takeover bid. Potential acquirers no longer restricted their targets to firms smaller than themselves, as some of Britain's largest firms discovered (e.g. Allied-Lyons, Distillers, Woolworth).

The leveraged bid (i.e. one based on heavy borrowing) was just one reason why smaller firms could buy firms much larger than themselves. The first leveraged bid in the UK was by Australia's Elders IXL for Allied-Lyons. A consortium of banks led by the US bank Citibank established the trend by backing Elders to the tune of £1.5 bn. The more conservative UK banks also started to finance bid activity. Leveraged bids thus became possible because borrowed money was readily available from lending institutions.

The introduction of success-geared fees for merchant bankers also encouraged smaller firms to mount larger bids by reducing the cost of failure. For example, Samuel Montagu, Argyll's merchant bank, agreed to accept a smaller commission if the bid for Distillers was unsuccessful. Otherwise Argyll's net costs would have been much more than £34 m, the net cost of the bid.

Another reason why size was no longer a deterrent in 1986 was that Britain had been in a long bull market for 4–5 years, and share prices had reached levels that imbued managements with confidence and the financial muscle to acquire companies, even those larger than themselves. The availability of funds and the bull market, however, do not explain *why* so many firms at the one time wanted to undertake major acquisitions.

Firms competing in a global industry (e.g. food, drinks) are very much aware of the benefits of economies of scale, but especially the need for a strong brand portfolio which determines their market share and rank *vis-à-vis* those of their rivals. Developing and launching products are costly in terms of resources and time, and risky too in that the product is untried in the market. Buying already successful brands is, therefore, a powerful attraction as the rewards are immediate. This desire to acquire market share is reinforced by the activities of rival companies. Today many of the world's largest global companies believe that 'big is better'. Thus, once one key player makes a major acquisition, the others follow suit either to catch up or maintain their leadership. This has occurred in a variety of sectors in which UK, or Anglo-Dutch, firms have been at the forefront of the acquisition trail at home or abroad (though not always successfully), for example advertising (Saatchi & Saatchi and WPP), chemicals (ICI), consumer products (Unilever), drinks (Allied-Lyons, Guinness, Grand Metropolitan), food (United Biscuits), publishing (Pearson) and telecommunications (GEC).

'Globalization' and the desire to become an industry giant would seem to be the primary motive underlying mega-bids such as those by Elders for Allied-Lyons, which itself acquired the drinks division of Canada's Hiram Walker; Guinness for Distillers; GEC for Plessey; and the contest between Nestlé and Jacobs Suchard for Rowntree.

Another major reason for takeovers has been that the management of the bidding company believes it can outperform the incumbent management of the target firm. This was the main reason behind Argyll's bid for Distillers, Dixons' for Woolworth, and BTR's for Pilkington Brothers.

Takeovers are also due to two factors that are often overlooked but which should never be underestimated: the human factor (managers enjoy the excitement and prestige of bidding) and pure fashion.

The players

Through a series of astute acquisitions, many companies have been transformed by the vision of their chairman or chief executive. The market capitalization and profits of firms such as Argyll, BTR, Dixons, Elders and Guinness all soared under the stewardship of their ambitious chairman and/or chief executive. Few executives can boast a track record to compare with that of James Gulliver, Sir Owen Green, Stanley Kalms, John Elliott and Ernest Saunders. Even among this elite group, the achievements of Saunders during his brief reign at Guinness were outstanding. Less than one year after his crowning achievement, the £2.5 bn takeover of Distillers, Saunders had been ousted from Guinness. In his desire to win the battle for corporate control, he had allegedly resorted to illegal means. In July 1988 he appeared at Bow Street magistrates' court, facing more than forty criminal charges and conducting his own defence, having been refused legal aid. In contrast, his defeated rival in the Distillers battle, James Gulliver, has voluntarily stepped down as the successful chief of Argyll. Gulliver, a University of Glasgow graduate and Visiting Professor, had just seen Argyll, owners of the Presto chain, become Britain's fourth largest grocery chain through the purchase of Safeway's UK stores. His mission accomplished, Gulliver required a fresh challenge and new business interests.

However, the dominant personality of the UK takeover scene remains Lord Hanson. Just as Saunders and Gulliver featured heavily, if for different reasons, in the business press in July 1988, so too did the 'uncanny restructurer' (Porter, 1987). Having acquired Imperial in 1986 for £2.6 bn, Hanson has recouped the purchase price by divesting units of the business. In July 1988 he sold HP Foods and Lea and Perrins to France's acquisitive BSN, and rumours abounded that Hanson was about to mount another mega-bid.

However, the personalities of the UK takeover scene are not restricted to the companies themselves. Merchant banks are very conscious of their position in the league tables, which are compiled to show which bank has won the most takeover business. In 1986, Morgan Grenfell was clearly number one, a position due on no small account to Roger Seelig and George Magan. The former has left the bank in the wake of the Guinness scandal, and is one of the brewer's 'war cabinet' facing criminal charges. Magan, on the other hand, has branched off to establish his own 'boutique bank'.

By 1988, the takeover stars in the City were Rupert Faurre of Samuel Montagu, John Thornton of Goldman Sachs, Bay Green of Hill Samuel and Nicholas Jones of Schroders. However, merchant banks have probably realized the dangers in cultivating the 'star system'.

These then are the main influences and some of the personalities that have been conspicuous in recent UK takeover activity. The trend and nature of such activity are reviewed in the following section.

1986–88: a merger boom?

In 1986, the year the Government announced its latest review of merger policy, 695 UK firms changed hands. According to commentators, Britain was in the grip of a merger boom. Phrases like 'merger fever' and 'merger mania' were some of the more colourful ones used to describe takeovers in 1986. However, these terms convey a slightly misleading description of the reality of recent developments.

In terms of the actual number of takeovers, the 1986 level of merger activity was *not* exceptionally high. In the 10 years before the 1973 oil crisis many more firms were acquired each year than in any year since then (see Figure 1.1). Between 1983 and 1986 a total of 2,184 British firms were taken over as against 4,092 during 1970–73 – a boom period in terms of the number of acquisitions. However, with 695 acquisitions in 1986, this was almost 50 per cent up on the 1985 level, and more than in any year since 1973 when there were more than 1,200.

Although the period 1980–86 did not see a peak in the number of mergers in the UK, expenditure on acquisitions has soared. Prior to 1984, the record level of expenditure was £2.53 bn set in 1972. This record was first broken in 1984 with bids concluded worth £5.47 bn, and again in 1985, when £7.09 bn was spent. Despite this significant increase in expenditure, in 1986 the value of UK acquisitions and mergers was £14.9 bn, more than double that of 1984 (see Figure 1.2).

Figures 1.1 and 1.2 reveal two important points about the frequency and value of UK acquisitions in 1986:

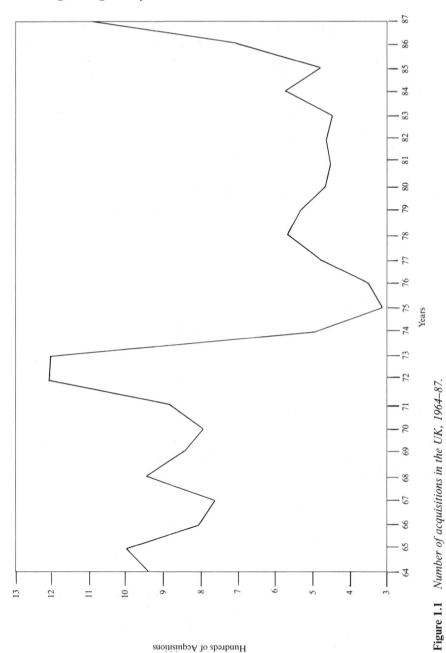

Figure 1.1 *Number of acquisitions in the UK, 1964–87.*

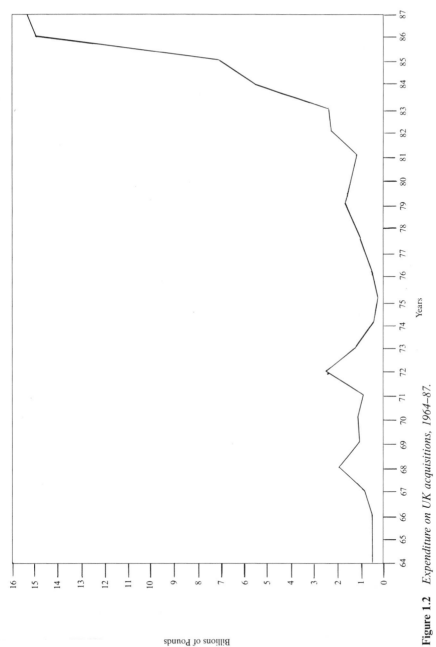

Figure 1.2 *Expenditure on UK acquisitions, 1964–87.*

Table 1.1   *The largest UK takeovers (to 30 November 1988)*

Year	Bidder	Target	Value (£ m)
1986	Hanson Trust	Imperial Group	2,660
1988	Nestlé	Rowntree	2,622
1986	Guinness	Distillers	2,531
1988	BP	Britoil	2,522
1986	Habitat Mothercare	British Home Stores	1,520
1986	Elders	Courage (Hanson Trust)	1,400
1983	BAT	Eagle Star	968
1987	TSB	Hill Samuel	777
1986	Vantona Viyella	Coats Patons	727
1988	Pleasurama	Mecca Leisure	725
1986	Dee Corporation	Fine Fare (Assoc. British Foods)	686
1987	Argyll	Safeway's UK stores	681
1986	British & Commonwealth	Exco	670
1984	BAT Industries	Hambro-Life	664
1983	BTR	Thomas Tilling	630
1985	Al Fayed Investment	House of Fraser	615
1985	ASDA	MFI	569
1987	British & Commonwealth	Mercantile House	564
1988	British Coal Pension	T R Ind & Gen. Trust	560
1986	Mercury Securities/Ackroyd & Smithers	Mercury International	551
1985	Burton Group	Debenhams	550
1987	Reed International	Octopus Publishing	547
1987	MEPC	Oldham Estate	504
1988	Sears	Freemans	477
1987	Compagnie du Midi	Equity & Law	458
1987	Tractabel & GBL	Contibel Holdings	448
1988	Lowndes	Harris Queensway	447
1987	Ferranti	Int. Signal & Control	425
1987	FKI	Babcock	416
1984	Standard Telephone	ICL	411
1984	Sun Alliance	Phoenix Assurance	397
1988	St Paul Companies	Minet Holdings	396
1984	Unilever	Brooke Bond	389
1988	British Commonwealth	Atlantic Computers	386
1973	Grand Metropolitan	Watney Mann	378
1988	British Gas	Acre Oil	370
1985	Guinness	Arthur Bell	356
1987	Equiticorp	Guinness Peat Group	353
1987	Mountleigh	Stockley	352
1987	WPP	JWT	352
1987	Next	Combined English Stores	324
1987	P & O	European Ferries	300

Sources: Acquisitions Monthly; Press reports.

Table 1.2 *Unsuccessful or withdrawn £500 m plus deals in 1986–88**

Year	Bidder	Target	Bid	Outcome
1986	United Biscuits	Imperial Group	2,508	Outbid
1986	Argyll	Distillers	2,495	Outbid
1988	Barker & Dobson	Dee Corporation	1,969	Rejected
1986	Elders	Allied-Lyons	1,870	Withdrawn
1986	Dixons	Woolworth	1,820	Rejected
1987	Mountleigh	Storehouse	1,800	Withdrawn
1988	Goodman Fielder Wattie	Ranks Hovis McDougall	1,700	Withdrawn
1986	Imperial Group	United Biscuits	1,300	Outbid
1986	Lloyds Bank	Standard Chartered	1,300	Rejected
1986	GEC	Plessey	1,170	Blocked by MMC
1987	BTR	Pilkington	1,156	Withdrawn
1987	Benlox Holdings	Storehouse	1,100	Rejected
1987	ABF	S. & W. Berisford	766	Rejected
1986	Gulf Resources	IC Gas	750	Rejected
1986	Rank Organization	Granada Group	740	Banned by IBA
1986	Dawson International	Coats Patons	634	Outbid
1987	Williams	Norcros	555	Rejected
1987	Anadrex Holdings	Mercantile House	530	Rejected

Source: Acquisitions Monthly.

*As at 30 November 1988.

(1) There were considerably fewer mergers in 1986 (695) than in the boom years of 1965 (1,000), 1972 (1,215) and 1973 (1,205).

(2) 1986 was a record year for expenditure on acquisitions (but this level was surpassed subsequently by expenditure in 1987).

Thus, a new expenditure record was set in 1986, not because there was a large number of acquisitions but mainly because of a small number of 'mega-mergers'.

The size of companies acquired (see Table 1.1) has been reflected in the growing size of bids, and thus the annual value of mergers and acquisitions in the UK. In 1983, the value of all UK acquisitions amounted to £2.3 bn, but just three years later this sum would not have bought either Distillers or Imperial. In 1986 the value of the three largest bids equalled the 1985 total. The incidence of mega-mergers has pushed

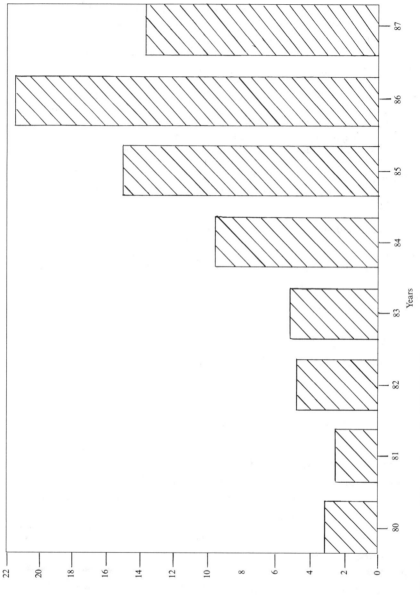

Figure 1.3   *Average acquisition value in the UK, 1980–87.*

up the average value of an acquisition from £3.1 m in 1980 to a high of £21.5 m in 1986 (Figure 1.3). The average value in 1986 would have been even higher had other mega-bids for UK companies been successful. Table 1.2 lists bids of more than £500 m which were either blocked by the Government, rejected or withdrawn.

In sum, 1986 merger activity in the UK had undergone a fundamental shift away from comparatively insignificant acquisitions towards mega-mergers. The *Financial Times*, in its annual retrospective look at UK takeovers in 1986, was characteristically accurate when it summed up the year in its headline 'A year of mega-bids and City scandals' (31 December 1986).

After BTR withdrew its bid for Pilkington in January 1987, there was almost a complete absence of mega-bids for UK companies until the final weeks of the year. This was not because of a lack of funds, but rather a preference for 'midi-bids' (i.e. £200–400 m) and acquisitions in the USA. Companies such as Bass, Blue Arrow, BTR, GEC, Grand Metropolitan, Hanson, Hawley, ICI, Ladbroke, National Westminster Bank, Pilkington and WPP all concluded major US acquisitions in the course of 1987. This lack of mega-bids and contested takeovers in the first six months of 1987 no doubt reflected the fact that since mid-1986 target companies had been more successful in warding off unwelcome bids (e.g. Woolworth, Pilkington, Norcros).

In the 12 months before the General Election in June 1987, advantage seemed to rest with the target company. The memory of the acrimonious bids in early 1986 and the Guinness scandal, plus political uncertainty, no doubt discouraged takeovers. However, in the second half of 1987, the former receded from the public gaze and the Election removed the latter. But the third quarter of 1987 did not see a return to the bid fever of 1986. With the stock-market crash of 'Black Monday' on 19 October, merger activity threatened to grind to a halt, and it was only in the final weeks of 1987 that merger activity resumed.

Although there was an absence of newsworthy major hostile/contested bids during the first nine months of 1987, one should not conclude that there had been a decline in merger activity. In fact quite the opposite was true; 216 firms were acquired in the first quarter of 1987, exactly double the number acquired (108) during the same period in 1986. In the second quarter of 1987, 294 companies were acquired, the highest quarterly total since the last quarter of 1973. Thus, 510 companies were acquired in the first half of 1987, only 185 fewer than in the whole of 1986. The value of acquisitions in the second quarter of 1987 was £4.68 bn, the second highest quarterly total on record, surpassed only by the £6.37 bn in the same quarter in 1986 which included the two highest ever deals (i.e. Hanson for Imperial, Guinness for Distillers).

Although there were no deals worth more than £400 m during the second quarter of 1987, more than half the total value was accounted for by eleven deals each worth more than £100 m. Six transactions were worth more than £200 m each.

During the third quarter of 1987, 353 companies were acquired, and in the final quarter a further 262 companies were acquired. Whereas 1986 had been an exceptional year in terms of the average value of takeovers, 1987 witnessed more deals than in any entire year since 1973 (see Figure 1.1). While there were some large bids, there were no major contested mega-bids until the final quarter when BP made a successful bid of £2.5 bn for Britoil, and Barker and Dobson bid £2 bn unsuccessfully for the Dee Corporation.

In 1988, a total of 1,338 companies were acquired, a 19 per cent increase on 1987. Post-crash there were, of course, fewer takeovers of listed companies owing to the difficulties of obtaining underwriting from the merchant banks. Companies which did succeed in making bids tended to have their own surplus funds and made offers of cash rather than shares. The major mega-bid of the period was the £2.6 bn bid by Nestlé for Rowntree concluded successfully in June. The latest mega-bids were the £1.7 bn bid in July by the Australian Goodman Fielder Wattie group for Ranks Hovis McDougall, subsequently withdrawn following referral to the Monopolies and Mergers Commission (MMC) by the Secretary of State for Trade and Industry, the record £2.9 bn bid in September by the South African-controlled Minorco group for Consolidated Gold Fields, subsequently referred to the MMC in October, the Elders IXL £1.6 bn bid for Scottish & Newcastle Breweries subsequently referred to the MMC in November and the GEC/Siemens £1.7 bn bid for Plessey.

This, then, is a picture of merger trends in the UK. But what has happened in other major industrial countries? The major developments in Continental Europe, Australasia, Japan and the United States are now briefly reviewed.

THE INTERNATIONAL SCENE

Continental Europe

A review of merger activity in many European countries is limited by a lack of official statistics, but it is clear that, like the UK, they too have witnessed a spate of major mergers and that many of these have been international takeovers. Unlike the UK, Continental European mergers have tended to be agreed mergers. Hostile takeovers are almost destined to fail because of the powerful influence of key equity shareholders or because of protective shareholding arrangements involving a distinction between voting and non-voting shares.

In *France*, the level of acquisition activity has been increasing with substantial increases in international takeovers; French companies acquired 194 foreign firms in 1987 compared to 134 in 1986 and 70 in 1985. French companies, like their UK rivals, have been responsible for some of the largest foreign takeovers of US companies, e.g. RCA's consumer electronics division by Thomson. However, the French have had to reconcile themselves to the other side of the coin, the fact that French firms will be acquired by foreigners. The French media speak of 'the Italian invasion' as Italy's largest companies and most prominent entrepreneurs have gained control, or a stake in key players, in the motor components (Valeo and Matra), perfume (Yves Saint Laurent) and sugar (Beghin-Sey) industries.

In the *Federal Republic of Germany* there were a record 887 acquisitions and mergers in 1987, including 405 involving foreign companies. The West Germans have coined their own phrase – 'elephant mergers' – to describe large-scale takeovers such as Daimler-Benz's purchase of AEG. West German companies have been major acquirers of US companies, e.g. Celanese by Hoechst and Inmont by BASF, but have also been attracted by other Continental European companies, e.g. SEAT of Spain by Volkswagen. At the same time, the number of West German acquisitions by foreign companies increased by almost 44 per cent between 1980 and 1987.

In *Italy*, while no official statistics are kept, it is clear that Italian companies have been active acquirers and at the centre of the rise in international merger activity. There has been an increasing number of foreign acquisitions by major companies such as Fiat, Ferruzzi, Olivetti and Pirelli. However, as in France, the Italians have seen some of their most prestigious firms pass into foreign ownership. Electrolux of Sweden acquired Zanussi, and only a counterbid by Fiat prevented Ford from acquiring Alfa Romeo.

In *The Netherlands*, by way of contrast, the number of mergers has declined from a peak of 620 in 1974 to 384 in 1987. However, in mid-1987 The Netherlands witnessed its first true, 'no holds barred' hostile takeover, when Elsevier bid for rival publishers Kluwer. But this bid failed, like every other hostile bid in The Netherlands in the past 30 years.

Protective shareholding arrangements and articles of association have served Dutch companies well in this regard. At the same time, Dutch companies have been active abroad and especially the largest companies such as Philips, Akzo, Royal Dutch Shell and Unilever.

Merger activity in *Sweden* was fairly steady in the 1970s but then peaked in the early 1980s. The number of acquisitions has fallen back from 1,037 in 1983, the peak year, to just 631 deals in 1987. However, many of these takeovers are very large and have been executed by a handful of multinationals, e.g. Electrolux, Volvo, Swedish Match, Aga, Asea. In contrast to the overall merger trend, the acquisition of Swedish companies by foreign companies has been increasing, and arousing some concern from the Swedish Government.

In contrast to The Netherlands and Sweden, the 1980s has seen a considerable increase in merger activity in *Switzerland*. Between 1973 and 1985 there were 1,574 takeovers, but 1,092 of these, or almost 70 per cent, have occurred in the 1980s. To put this in perspective, between 1973 and 1979 there was an average of 69 mergers per year, compared to an average of 184 per year in the period 1980–85. Many of these involved foreign takeovers by the largest Swiss multinationals including Nestlé, Brown-Boveri, Ciba-Geigy and Sandoz.

Whether it has been the size of takeover bids or the level of foreign acquisitions, the current spate of acquisitions and mergers has aroused increasing concern in Continental European countries.

Australasia

In *Australia*, as in many other countries, there have been several large takeovers in sectors ranging from the media to mining, and especially in the food and drink sector. Following a sharp increase in merger activity in the early 1970s, it has fluctuated since then. But in 1983–84 there were 121 deals, almost double the previous year's level, and this level of activity has been maintained since that time. In contrast, there has been a steady increase in merger activity in *New Zealand* ever since 1976–77, when the Commerce Commission began considering merger proposals. In 1977–78 there were only 48 mergers, but by 1988 there had been a tenfold increase in merger activity.

Of particular recent interest, and concern to potential target companies, has been the wave of hostile bids for foreign, and especially UK, companies by antipodean entrepreneurs such as Rupert Murdoch, John Elliott, Alan Bond and Ron Brierley.

Japan

A common misconception is that acquisitions and mergers do not occur in Japan. In fact, in every year since 1970 there have never been fewer than 1,000 such deals concluded in any individual year. In 1987, the peak year, there were more than 2,200 deals. However, many mergers in Japan involve business transfers as opposed to combinations of corporate entities. More significant, however, is that Japanese culture frowns on hostile takeovers. Friendly mergers are the norm and often occur as a result of the initiative of a third party such as a bank or other institutional shareholder. Nevertheless, hostile bids are not unknown in Japan.

In 1986, the first-ever foreign hostile bid was mounted by Trafalgar-Glen, an Anglo-American holding company, for Minebea, the ball-bearing manufacturer. Observers question whether the bid was ever a serious proposition, or merely a means of raising a quick profit. 1986 also saw Dainippon Ink/Chemicals pay $560 m for the graphics division of Sun Chemical of the USA, a record American takeover by a Japanese company until Sony bought CBS Records for $2 bn in the autumn of 1987. A new record was set in the spring of 1988 when Bridgestone paid $2.6 bn for Firestone.

However, not all Japanese bids for US companies have met with success. In 1986, Fujitsu was forced to abort its bid for America's Fairchild Semiconductor which was owned by Schlumberger of France. Officials in Washington were already angered by Japan's alleged breaches of the semiconductor trade pact between the two countries signed in the summer of 1986. They baulked at the idea of Fairchild coming under Japanese control, and the US and Japanese companies bowed to political pressure and abandoned the proposed acquisition.

It is not just in Europe that an open-door policy to foreign acquisitions is under scrutiny. However, the extent of foreign ownership is certainly not the major issue to have emerged from America's merger boom.

The United States of America

Only a few statistics are necessary to stress the scale of merger activity in the USA. In the four years of 'merger mania' during 1983–86, some 12,200 US companies and corporate divisions changed hands in transactions worth at least $490 bn. There were 4,024 mergers and acquisitions in 1986 alone. Were the 1986 rate of mergers and acquisitions to continue every US public company would have new owners by the year 2001.

According to W.T. Grimm, the Chicago-based firm, in 1987 the value of mergers and acquisitions in the USA was $163.7 bn against $173.1 bn in 1986. As in the UK, expenditure in the USA has risen dramatically during the 1980s. In 1982, just $53.7 bn was spent on acquisitions and mergers. Between 1984 and 1985 there had been a sharp increase in the number of billion dollar acquisitions. In 1984 there were only 18 such deals, worth some $58.1 bn, but in 1985 the figures had soared to 36 and $92.7 bn respectively. In 1986, the number of these mega-deals slipped to 18 with a total value of $58.1 bn. In 1987, the number returned to 36 with expenditure exceeding $66 bn.

The US takeover boom has been fuelled by 'junk bonds' which allow firms with a low credit rating to borrow much more than their credit rating would normally allow. These loans are clearly high risk and this is reflected in the interest charged to the borrowers. Not surprisingly, economists are gravely concerned that the US economy is becoming increasingly vulnerable because a rise in interest rates could have catastrophic consequences. Such an increase would be almost unavoidable, for example, if there were an economic downturn such as that in 1981 which led to record high interest rates of over 20 per cent. And of course, a higher interest rate is levied on 'junk bonds'. As Felix Rohatyn of Lazard Frères has said, corporations are liquidating their future for today.

The relationship between junk bonds and the Boesky scandal, among others, was investigated in 1987 by the Senate's Banking Committee led by Senator Proxmire. This committee heard Rohatyn refer to the 'cancer of greed' which had taken hold of America's financial community. His observation would have provoked outrage 12 months earlier, but since the US Securities and Exchange Commission charged Dennis Levine with insider trading on 12 May 1986, many of the richest and best-known players in the securities industry have confessed to their crimes.

It may yet be too early to assess fully the impact of the recent stream of mergers on the US economy, but already many prominent US politicians and business people have demanded legislation to curb the excesses of takeover battles. For example, Congress has flirted with the idea of outlawing 'greenmail', whereby a company buys its own shares at a hefty premium from the raider(s) in exchange for an agreement to abort the takeover bid. Anglo-French financier, Sir James Goldsmith, abandoned his bid for Goodyear only after he made a massive profit from a 'greenmail' payment. A bitter Robert Mercer, Chairman of Goodyear, called on the Reagan Administration to toughen up its takeover laws. He takes a dim view of raiders whom he denounces as 'economic terrorists'. Similar sentiments are echoed by Lee Iacocca in his latest book *Talking*

Straight (1988). No doubt the raiders would remind them that one man's terrorist is another man's freedom fighter.

Raiders argue that they, as active investors, weed out poor management. They believe that management often protects its own interests at the expense of shareholders, the company owners. Critics allege that rather than improve competitiveness, raiders have forced management to abandon long-term planning and adopt an unhealthy concentration on a short-term horizon.

The raiders for their part are strongly opposed to 'poison pills' and 'shark repellents' with which potential takeover targets try to become takeover-proof by cancelling voting rights on shares, taking on heavy debts, disposing of or locking up prize assets or 'crown jewels', and even devising mechanisms to trigger off automatic liquidation in the event of a hostile bid. Some firms have, for example, thwarted a takeover bid only by divesting operations which were considered crucial to corporate development and expansion.

SUMMARY AND CONCLUSIONS

After more than three years of hectic merger activity, there is no sign yet of the end of the boom in mega-mergers. Even the 'Black Monday' stock-market crash of October 1987 has failed to have any long-term impact. Undaunted, companies across the globe are continuing to consolidate their core businesses through related acquisitions.

In 1987, a record \$40 bn was spent on US takeovers by foreign companies. While 1988 may not see this record broken, the emergence of cash-rich Japanese giants is likely to boost the value of US assets bought by foreigners. Similarly, the Europeans will continue to buy attractive business units to increase their market share in what is still the world's largest single market.

However, theoretically in 1992 Europe will supersede the USA. The idea of a single market of 320 million consumers is being heavily sold to European companies by third-party acquisition specialists. National champions face the reality of buy or be bought. In order to protect themselves and ensure their competitiveness, more and more European firms are engaging in international acquisitions in Europe and the USA. For example, Pearson, owner of the *Financial Times*, has bought *Les Echos* and *Cinco Dias*, the leading business newspapers in France and Spain respectively, as well as Addison-Wesley in the USA, and has also completed a share swap with the Dutch publisher Elsevier as a protective measure against predators.

There can be little doubt that mega-mergers will continue. No doubt many more such deals will have been concluded between the time of writing (November 1988) and the publication of this book. Indeed, any UK firm owning a range of best-selling brands is a likely takeover target. As more and more prestigious UK firms come under foreign ownership, it is likely that there will be a political backlash. But will it still be Pearson's *Financial Times* that makes the report?

In the next chapter, the UK regulatory environment is examined with particular reference to merger policy and the roles of the Office of Fair Trading, the Monopolies and Mergers Commission and the Secretary of State for Trade and Industry.

2

The Policy-Makers and Regulators: Merger Control

Merger control in a statutory context was first introduced in 1965 by the Monopolies and Mergers Act, but the passing of the Fair Trading Act 1973 represented a new era in merger control. The 1973 Act provides for the setting up of the Office of Fair Trading (OFT) with the appointment of a Director General (DG) and gives clearly defined roles to the DG, the Monopolies and Mergers Commission (MMC) and the Secretary of State for Trade and Industry. The DG advises the Secretary of State, and the Commission investigates merger proposals referred by the Secretary of State, who decides on the basis of an MMC recommendation whether or not the merger is against 'the public interest'.

THE SYSTEM OF MERGER CONTROL

Under the Fair Trading Act 1973, the Director General of the OFT is required to scrutinize all mergers in which the newly formed enterprise would have a 25 per cent market share of a particular product (goods or service), or where the assets of the target company exceed £30 m, the new threshold set after two amendments to the 1973 Act. The majority of mergers are, of course, excluded because they do not exceed either of these two critical thresholds. At the same time, many potential mergers are deterred by the prospect of being referred to the MMC and are thus ultimately blocked on competition grounds.

In the course of its investigation, the OFT is at liberty to offer 'confidential guidance' to individual companies on the question of whether a referral recommendation is likely, and if so on what grounds. In 1984 Norman Tebbit, Secretary of State for Trade and Industry, stipulated that the Government's policy would be 'to make references primarily on competition grounds'. In practice, it would seem that competition effects are assessed in terms of market power in the UK market and include consideration of competition from imports. However, the precise grounds for referring a merger to the MMC are not defined by the Fair Trading Act thus giving the Minister, the Secretary of State for Trade and Industry, considerable discretion in the exercise of his or her power.

Once the OFT has completed its review of a proposed or completed merger, the DG advises the Secretary of State on whether a referral should be made to the Monopolies and Mergers Commission. The Secretary of State is free to accept or reject this advice, and there have been a number of occasions when the Minister has chosen to reject the DG's recommendation. Only the Secretary of State can make a referral to the MMC.

Once a referral has been made, the MMC examines the case to see if the merger is likely to be against the public interest. In the meantime the current bid lapses but may be renewed on a favourable outcome. A report is published on all referrals unless the bid is withdrawn.

An MMC investigation can last as long as six months. Once complete, the MMC submits its report, including its verdict on whether a merger should be allowed to proceed or be prohibited, to the OFT and the Secretary of State. If the MMC concludes that a merger should be permitted, the Secretary of State has no power of veto, but where it decides that a merger should be prohibited, the Secretary of State is not obliged to accept its findings. Since 1965 the Secretary of State has very rarely overruled the Commission (e.g. in 1982 Charter Consolidated was allowed to acquire Anderson Strathclyde, even though the Commission had concluded by a 4–2 majority that the acquisition was against the public interest).

When the MMC decides that a merger is against the public interest, the Secretary of State has the power to block or clear the merger. This then is the UK merger control process. However, in order to understand more clearly the issues involved, it is necessary to examine in greater depth the roles of the main participants in the merger review process. Those involved seek to ensure that mergers against the public interest are prohibited (though statute does not define what constitutes the public interest), but they are not responsible for policing corporate conduct during takeover battles. Responsibility for this lies with the Stock Exchange and the Panel on Takeovers and Mergers (the Takeover Panel).

THE OFFICE OF FAIR TRADING

The Office of Fair Trading (OFT) employs only a small group of people in its mergers section. The OFT is expected to monitor merger activity.

Despite the obvious staff shortage, companies are not obliged to inform the OFT of a proposed merger even though imposing such a requirement on companies would not appear excessive, and would allow OFT staff to concentrate on their primary duty – vetting mergers. Not surprisingly, Sir Gordon Borrie, DG since 1976, has sought more staff. One reason is that it has proved impossible always to provide a recommendation before a bid's first closing date, as is the custom. Seven bids have slipped past the first closing date, including Dixons' £1.6 bn bid for Woolworth. This is hardly surprising given the demands placed on the OFT.

Table 2.1 provides a statistical record of the total number of merger proposals falling within the scope of the 1973 Fair Trading Act. The value of assets bid for in 1986 was the highest-ever level, up 114 per cent on the 1985 total. In 1987, the OFT examined some 321 cases, compared with 313 in 1986, which was a 67 per cent increase on the 192 cases in 1985. Of the 321 cases which were examined by the OFT, 6 were referred, on Sir Gordon's advice, to the MMC, compared with 13 in 1986.

In 1987 the OFT examined 15 proposals in which the gross assets of the target company exceeded £1 bn, compared with 29 such cases in 1986

Table 2.1 *Number and value of merger proposals falling within the scope of the 1973 Fair Trading Act, 1973–87*

Year	Number of proposals covered by Fair Trading Act (all cases)	Proposals covered by Fair Trading Act (all cases, assets bid for, £ m)
1973	114	4,878
1974	85	7,621
1975	116	5,786
1976	163	4,123
1977	194	4,675
1978	229	11,999
1979	257	13,140
1980	182	22,289
1981	164	43,597
1982	190	25,939
1983	192	45,495
1984	259	80,688
1985	192	57,488
1986	313	123,331
1987	321	121,911

Source: Office of Fair Trading.

Note: The assets criterion was revised from £5 m to £15 m in April 1980, and to £30 m in July 1984.

(Office of Fair Trading, 1986, 1987). In his 1986 annual report, Sir Gordon explained that apart from the considerable rise in the number of cases.

> There was, indeed, a hidden extra in that many of last year's [i.e. 1986's] cases called for more detailed economic analysis or raised new points of law or procedure.

The OFT had an annual budget of £8.7 m for the financial year ending 31 March 1987. Of this amount, the merger-vetting section received only 5 per cent to cover its work (Office of Fair Trading, 1986). Despite the limited resources, and the lack of a pre-notification requirement, the OFT normally takes only four to six weeks to advise the Secretary of State on 'substantial cases' (Borrie, 1987b).

In a speech to the Finance Houses Association in 1986, Sir Gordon defended UK merger policy. He claimed that far from clouding policy, the wave of mega-mergers had been illuminating. He argued that while 'existing policy and procedures should be thoroughly examined in the light of experience', in the Government's review of competition and merger policy 'it [is] quite wrong to suggest that recent events have somehow left existing policy and procedures in a state of chaos' (Borrie, 1986a).

Apart from the repackaging of takeover bids following consultation with the OFT, two other aspects of takeovers have been clarified by recent cases. The first is the grounds on which the decision is taken to refer a case to the MMC. In July 1984, the Secretary of State for Trade and Industry affirmed that the primary ground for referral was concern that competition in a particular market may be significantly reduced. As Sir Gordon stresses, ' "primary" does not mean "exclusive" ' (Borrie, 1986a). Thus the OFT recommended a referral for the £1.8 bn bid by Australia's Elders IXL for Allied-Lyons, not because it posed any threat on competition grounds, but because it was a highly leveraged bid. In Sir Gordon's words, it 'demonstrated in an extreme form the new trend to mount bids with borrowed money' (Borrie, 1986a).

Second, in such cases where two companies are bidding for the same firm, the OFT may decide to refer just one bid. The other bid will *not* automatically be referred. Therefore there is an advantage to the firm whose bid does not arouse the OFT's concern. Target company shareholders are not guaranteed a choice in such circumstances.

THE MONOPOLIES AND MERGERS COMMISSION (MMC)

The Monopolies Commission was established by Act of Parliament in 1948, but it was another 25 years before its name was changed to the Monopolies and Mergers Commission, in acknowledgement of its new powers, granted in 1965, to investigate mergers.

The chairman and members of the Commission are appointed by the Secretary of State for Trade and Industry. Members come from a variety of different professional backgrounds. In recent years, members have included accountants, economists, engineers, industrialists, management consultants, trade unionists and former civil servants. With such diverse backgrounds, the Secretary of State has to strike a delicate balance in appointments to ensure that the views of no one occupation or interest group predominate.

Commission members have supporting staff, including accountants and economists, to assist them in their investigations. This support is invaluable, as members normally continue to perform their own day-to-day business or professional duties even when they are involved in an investigation. Given their other commitments and duties, it is little wonder that an investigation by the MMC can last as long as six months.

Table 2.2 shows that thirteen bids were referred to the MMC in 1986 – more than in any previous year during the 1980s, and more than in 1984 and 1985 combined. Of the thirteen, seven bids were abandoned during the MMC's investigation, three were blocked, and three were cleared and

Table 2.2 *Outcome of takeover bids referred to the Monopolies and Mergers Commission, 1980–88*

Year	No. of referrals	No. abandoned during investigation	Pending	Blocked	Cleared		
					Failed takeover	Successful takeover	Proposal abandoned
1980	5	1	–	1	0	3	0
1981	8	1	–	5	0	2	0
1982	10	2	–	4	2	2	0
1983	9	2	–	4	3	0	0
1984	4	1	–	0	2	1	0
1985	6	2	–	0	1	1	2
1986	13	7*	–	3	0	3	0
1987	6	0	–	3	0	3	0
1988	6	2	2	2	–	–	–

Source: Office of Fair Trading, Annual reports of the Director General of Fair Trading.

* Includes the original bid by Guinness for Distillers which was repackaged to avoid a referral and eventually proved successful in beating Argyll to win Distillers. Also includes Imperial's bid for United Biscuits (UB). UB subsequently bid for Imperial but lost to Hanson Trust.

Table 2.3 *Monopolies and Mergers Commission investigations (excluding newspaper merger references), 1984–87*

Bidder	Target	Outcome
1984		
Lonrho	House of Fraser	Not against the public interest
Scottish & Newcastle	J. W. Cameron	Proposal abandoned
Dee Corporation	Booker McConnell	Not against the public interest
British Electric Traction	Initial	Not against the public interest
1985		
Imperial Group	Permaflex	Proposal abandoned
Scottish & Newcastle	Matthew Brown	Not against the public interest
British Telecom	Mitel	Against the public interest but allowed to proceed by Secretary of State
McCorquodale	Richard Clay	Proposal abandoned
Elders	Allied-Lyons	Not against the public interest but proposal abandoned
BET	SGB	Not against the public interest but proposal abandoned
1986		
GEC	Plessey	Against the public interest
Imperial Group	United Biscuits	Bid initially referred then laid aside and UB bid unsuccessfully for Imperial
Guinness	Distillers	Bid initially referred but laid aside and new bid launched
Cope Allman	Firth Cleveland Strip	Proposal abandoned
Norton Opax	McCorquodale	Not against the public interest
Hillsdown Holdings	British Sugar	Proposal abandoned
Tate & Lyle	S. & W. Berisford	Against the public interest
London International	Wedgwood	Proposal abandoned
P & O	European Ferries	Not against the public interest
Ferruzi	S. & W. Berisford	Against the public interest
Trusthouse Forte	Assets of Hanson Trust (i.e. Imperial Group's restaurants)	Not against the public interest

Bidder	Target	Outcome
Strong & Fisher	Garnar Booth	Proposal abandoned
Gulf Resources & Chemical Corp.	Imperial Continental Gas Association	Proposal abandoned
1987		
Co-operative Wholesale Society	House of Fraser Funeral Division	Against the public interest
Swedish Match	Wilkinson Sword from Allegheny Int.	Not against the public interest
MAI PLC	London & Continental Advertising Holdings	Against the public interest
British Airways	British Caledonian	Not against the public interest
Warner Communications	Chappell & Co.	Not against the public interest
Book Club Associates	Leisure Circle	Against the public interest

Sources: Office of Fair Trading, Annual Reports of the Director General of Fair Trading; Monopolies and Mergers Commission.

eventually resulted in a merger. Six bids were referred in 1987; three were blocked and the other three resulted in successful takeovers.

Between 1984 and 1987, twenty-nine cases were referred to the MMC. Ten were abandoned (including Guinness's original bid for Distillers and Imperial Group's bid for United Biscuits, which was abandoned and the roles reversed). Six bids were blocked in the four years, and all of these were cases referred in 1986 and 1987. As Table 2.3 reveals, these were: in 1986, GEC's bid for Plessey, and bids for S. & W. Berisford from Tate & Lyle, and Ferruzi, the rapidly expanding Italian group; and in 1987, the Co-operative Wholesale Society's bid for House of Fraser's Funeral Division, MAI's bid for London and Continental Advertising and the Book Club Associates bid for Leisure Circle. Table 2.3 provides a complete listing of the twenty-nine cases referred to the MMC from 1984 to 1987, and the outcome of each case.

Prior to 1987, all of the cases referred to the MMC were done so prior to the consummation of the merger. In July 1987, Lord Young, the Secretary of State for Trade and Industry, on the advice of the OFT, took the unusual step of referring two cases in which the merger had already been completed – one of them almost six months earlier (N.B. a completed acquisition cannot be referred to the MMC once six months have elapsed since the deal has been concluded).

One of the two referrals was Swedish Match's £99.2 m acquisition of Wilkinson Sword from Allegheny International of the USA in March 1987. This deal brought together the world's two largest producers of matches, and resulted in Swedish Match controlling 80 per cent of the UK match market worth £100 m at retail prices. The second acquisition referred to the MMC was the £36 m deal in which MAI, the financial services group, bought London and Continental Advertising Holdings. MAI won this contested bid on 8 January 1987 and the takeover united Britain's two largest roadside poster contractors. Why, one may ask, were these deals not referred to the MMC before the acquisitions actually occurred?

The Swedish Match acquisition was referred after the deal had been concluded because the Swedish company and the US seller presented the OFT with a *fait accompli*. The OFT only knew of the deal after the transaction had been completed. In October 1987 the MMC concluded the merger was not against the public interest.

The MAI deal had been cleared by the OFT in December 1986, when MAI undertook to sell some of the sites of the proposed group to two other contractors. Lord Young's decision followed OFT advice that MAI had not sold poster sites exactly as promised to the OFT, even though it had met the OFT's fundamental requirement that it reduce its UK market share to 28 per cent. The MMC subsequently blocked this deal.

On only one other occasion had plea bargaining with the OFT led to a bid not being referred and an eventual takeover. This was Guinness's bid for Distillers. At the time this decision, or 'corporate gerrymandering' as an Argyll executive dubbed it, was strongly criticized. Lord Young's decision to refer MAI shows that commitments given to the OFT must be strictly adhered to, and that any deviations will not be tolerated, even if the net result is the same. Of course, an alternative interpretation of Lord Young's decision is that the Government has decided to discourage the whole practice of plea-bargaining with the OFT.

Lord Young ordered the MMC to report on Swedish Match within three months, and MAI within four months. In August 1987, the £237 m agreed takeover of British Caledonian by British Airways was referred to the MMC. Once again, Lord Young recognized the advantages of a quick decision by the MMC, and instructed it to report within three months – normally an MMC investigation can take up to six months – with the MMC advising that the takeover was not against the public interest.

In the first half of 1988, three bids were referred: one was abandoned during investigation (Hanson for George Armitage), while reports on the other two – Mitek for Gang-mail Systems and the Kuwait Investment

Office for a stake in BP – concluded that the Mitek bid was against the public interest and that the Kuwait Investment Office stake should be reduced from 21.7 to 9.9 per cent. More recently up to 30 November 1988, Lord Young has referred the following bids: Goodman Fielder Wattie for Ranks Hovis McDougall (bid subsequently abandoned), Minorco for Consolidated Gold Fields and Elders IXL for Scottish and Newcastle Breweries.

THE SECRETARY OF STATE FOR TRADE AND INDUSTRY

Since 1965 only two MMC verdicts have been overruled by the Minister. It must be stressed that there are two restrictions on the Minister's powers. The first relates to the size of the Commission's majority. A proposed merger can only be blocked if the Commission decides by a two-thirds majority that it can be expected to operate against the public interest. Second, if the Commission decides that 'a merger does not operate, or can be expected not to operate, against the public interest', the Minister has no power to act.

Since the Conservatives' June 1983 election victory there have been no fewer than five Secretaries of State for Trade and Industry (Cecil Parkinson, Norman Tebbit, Leon Brittan, Paul Channon and Lord Young), with Sir Alex Fletcher, Geoffrey Pattie and Michael Howard respectively taking charge temporarily when Parkinson, Tebbit and Channon were unable to act, being involved with personal matters.

Despite the rapid turnover in Ministers, merger policy has been consistently applied since it was reviewed in 1984. This represents an improvement on the early 1980s. Between 1981 and 1983, on a number of occasions (e.g. Lonrho's bid for House of Fraser) the Government rejected OFT recommendations, and on one occasion (i.e. Charter Consolidated's 1982 bid for Anderson Strathclyde) it even rejected the conclusion of the MMC. In this celebrated case, Professor Andrew Bain resigned from the MMC in protest at the Government's action.

At that time, UK merger policy was not only unpredictable, but apparently in disarray. The reputations of the OFT and MMC had been badly bruised, and a government review to clarify merger policy was essential. This review was completed by July 1984. The then Minister, Norman Tebbit, concluded that current legislation was functioning satisfactorily, and clarified the grounds for referral: 'My policy has been and will continue to be to make references primarily on competition grounds.' Since Tebbit issued this statement, his successors have all abided by the principle that bids should be referred to the MMC 'primarily', though not exclusively, on competition grounds. However, there have been a few exceptions (see following section). Nevertheless, merger policy has become much more predictable. This is clearly desirable, and the decision *not* to refer to the MMC (despite intense political lobbying) the bid by BTR, one of Britain's largest and most successful conglomerates, for Pilkington, the glassmaker, has underlined the Government's commitment to refer bids 'primarily' on competition grounds.

However, there has still been the odd occasion when the Minister has rejected OFT advice, and not referred a bid to the MMC. Throughout 1985, OFT advice was accepted by the Minister, but in 1986 it was twice rejected. Sir Gordon Borrie had recommended that the takeover of Screen Entertainments, which included the ABC cinema chain, by the Cannon Group, the US film production and distribution company, should be referred to the MMC. He believed that since the takeover would create by far the largest cinema chain in the UK, the MMC should investigate to see if the takeover was in the public interest. Paul Channon rejected his advice, and Cannon bought Screen Entertainments from its owner of all of seven days, Australia's Bond Corporation. This Australian brewing, media and energy group had just bought Screen Entertainments from Thorn-EMI for £125 m. Cannon was prepared to pay £175 m to relieve Alan Bond of his new investment. Bond's seven-day ownership of the large UK cinema chain had netted him a cool £50 m profit.

Channon also gave the go-ahead to Owens-Corning, the US building materials group, to acquire two subsidiaries of Pilkington Brothers. He once again rejected the arguments of Sir Gordon, who believed that a takeover would reduce European competition to two key players, i.e. the new group, and Saint Gobain of France, who would be able to exercise strong influence over fibreglass prices. The OFT stated that this dominance would be an effective barrier to entry by other firms, and that competition in the UK market in particular would be weak because the Owens-Corning group's market share would be double that of Saint Gobain. However, Channon contended that the potential detriment to competition was not serious enough 'to outweigh the employment and efficiency benefits to be gained from the strengthening of the UK fibreglass industry likely to result'.

Grounds for referral to the Monopolies and Mergers Commission

For the past four years (i.e. since July 1984), UK merger policy has been based on Norman Tebbit's view that referrals to the MMC should be made *primarily* on competition grounds. In a recent speech at Glasgow University, Sir Gordon Borrie (1987b) explained that since Tebbit's clarification of merger policy, virtually all cases referred to the MMC posed a possible threat to competition. The exceptions have been Elders' bid for Allied-Lyons and the bid by Gulf Resources, a small US energy group, for IC Gas, because of the high amount of borrowing required to finance them, and the Hillsdown bid for S. & W. Berisford, the parent company of British Sugar, 'referred because of the importance of British Sugar in the context of the CAP sugar regime'. In addition, the acquisition of London and Continental Advertising Holdings by MAI was referred because MAI had not exactly complied with its plea-bargaining undertakings to the OFT.

As regards competition grounds, companies and their advisers have discovered that a referral can almost certainly be avoided by consulting the OFT and divesting the appropriate business units, following its advice, so that the OFT will not recommend referral. If this option was not available to companies, it is likely that the MMC would face the prospect of conducting more investigations. Apart from the costs involved, this would slow down rather than accelerate the investigations of the Commission, which are already deemed by many to take too long.

UK merger policy may be effective in that those cases which reduce competition to an unacceptable level are referred to the MMC and subsequently prohibited. However, it could be argued that it does fail to take account of conglomerate mergers which do not have a direct effect on competition but increase the concentration of economic power. Current merger policy does not address the issues related to aggregate concentration and so diversified firms, such as BTR, Hanson Trust and the mini-conglomerates, can continue to expand unchecked. While the shareholders of these companies have certainly reaped benefits, there are also potential detrimental effects which may arise when conglomerates become too large to be managed effectively or lack sufficient synergy of operations to justify their existence.

Under current legislation, the fate of virtually all mergers with no detrimental competitive impact is decided by market forces – or, in other words, the shareholders, and the institutional shareholders in particular. But it may be questioned whether investor decisions to buy or sell shares at a particular price necessarily achieve the most efficient deployment and development of assets from an economy-wide or national perspective.

It has been suggested by some, including Sir Gordon Borrie, that, in the case of mega-mergers especially, companies ought to be made to show that their proposed bid will produce positive benefits, and not simply indicate that it will not be against the public interest. Others would argue, however, that only the owners of the target company, the shareholders, have the right to decide whether or not a bid is acceptable.

Grounds for referral: alternative views

Had the Conservatives failed to win the June General Election in 1987, it is certain that Labour would have changed UK merger policy. Only a year earlier, on 5 June 1986, the Government itself had initiated a review of 'both the scope for changes in [merger] policy under present legislation and the desirability of changes in the law'. Currently, the law does not require the bidder to prove that a merger is in the public interest. A merger may only be stopped if the Government decides it is against the public interest.

The Labour Party argues that the onus of proof should be shifted to the bidder, so that it would have to persuade the MMC that a merger was in the public interest, instead of the MMC proving it was against it. Roy Hattersley, Deputy Leader of the Labour Party, has proposed too that any merger which would create an undertaking with assets worth more than £15 m should be pre-notified to the Office of Fair Trading. The OFT would then have 30 days in which to decide whether to refer the merger for investigation by the Monopolies and Mergers Commission. Moreover, pre-notification would be required for mergers covering more than 25 per cent of a regional or national market, or those involving a foreign stake of over 15 per cent.

According to Bryan Gould, Shadow Spokesman for Trade and Industry, merger policy has to recognize the importance not just of the national market, but of regional and international markets. Local monopolies should be prohibited and those sectors identified in which international market share is paramount. Of course, the international market should not be an automatic substitute for the domestic market, but merger policy must recognize this international dimension. Gould also argues that the Government should refer bids where the buyer plans to rationalize the acquisition and the motive for the acquisition is to reduce competition. In such cases the interests of the acquirer may be at odds with the national interest, and accordingly such bids merit careful scrutiny. Gould also believes that employees' interests are not adequately safeguarded. He recognizes that merger policy cannot be used to protect jobs at risk, but when a merger would lead to job losses the case should be automatically referred to the MMC (interview with Bryan Gould, 3 March 1986).

The view that the burden of proof be shifted is a popular one to which both the SLD and SDP parties also adhere. Sir Gordon Borrie himself believes that 'a change in the burden of proof would certainly blow away the froth from the "frothy and hysterical merger boom"'. In a recent speech, having taken the precaution of stating the argument in hypothetical terms, he suggested that participants in mergers above a certain size might be required 'to demonstrate positive *benefits* flowing from it if the merger is to be cleared' and 'be forced to assert the expected benefits of the merger and to answer all allegations of potential detriments (including regional detriments) or they would fail to pass the test' (Borrie, 1986b).

One particular aspect that has aroused controversy in the context of alternative grounds for referral is the regional dimension. In the past few years, many of Scotland's largest companies have been taken over (e.g. House of Fraser, Arthur Bell, Coats Patons, Britoil and, most controversially of all, Distillers) and the locus of decision-making transferred, usually to the south-east of England. This trend has caused concern north of the border, recently revived by the Elders IXL bid in October 1988 for Scottish and Newcastle Breweries. The Scottish Council for Development and Industry (1986) argues that 'there should be a requirement on the parties to a merger to consult the appropriate government body on the regional development implications of the proposal'. Debate as to whether merger policy should be used as a surrogate branch of industrial/regional policy underlay much of the controversy in BTR's bid for Pilkington, which is based in north-west England.

According to a paper commissioned by the Scottish Council for Development and Industry, 'changes are urgently required in present competition policy ... "the regional interest" should justifiably be regarded as one of the major criteria determining the desirability or otherwise of merger/takeover proposals' (Buxton, 1986).

ISSUES RELATING TO MERGER POLICY

UK merger policy is three-tiered with the OFT, MMC and Secretary of State for Trade and Industry all playing key, though quite different, roles. The Director General of the OFT advises the Minister, the MMC investigates merger proposals referred by the Minister, and the Minister decides. Since 1984 these three main parties in UK merger policy have avoided the controversial disagreements of the early 1980s, and merger policy has become more predictable, though it is still high on the political agenda. This statutory framework is supported by self-regulatory bodies – the Stock Exchange and the Panel on Takeovers and Mergers – which control the corporate conduct of takeover bids.

Several issues can be identified in the context of regulation. The first concerns the notification of mergers to the OFT. Given the paucity of resources at its disposal, there is a strong case for the OFT to receive, on a compulsory basis, notification of proposed mergers above a certain size, before and after these mergers have been concluded. It appears too that there is some support for the view that, in respect of referred bids, the burden of proof should be shifted from the MMC to the bidder, especially for mega-mergers. In such cases the parties involved would be compelled to identify the expected benefits and counter all allegations of potential adverse consequences.

There is also some concern to consider more fully the question of competition in the wider international and EC contexts rather than just that of the UK domestic market. Furthermore, many economists now argue that market share is only one measure of market power, and not necessarily the most important. According to economic theory, the most important criterion in deciding whether a merger is anti-competitive is not the market share of the merged enterprise, but whether the merger would prohibit newcomers from the market. If barriers to entry are weak, then in principle even a monopoly cannot exploit its dominant position for fear of attracting competitors. Where barriers to entry are high, then maintaining competition between players already in the industry is much more important.

Barriers to exit from an industry, such as specialized assets, assets with low liquidation values, strategic interconnections, government and social restrictions, are also important. If these are high, firms will be reluctant to enter the market. Thus strong exit barriers afford protection to those already in the industry. On the other hand, weak barriers to exit encourage a flow of arrivals and departures, thus those permanently based within the industry must be competitive and consumers are not disadvantaged.

It is vital that the correct balance is struck between competitive effects in the domestic and international markets in deciding whether to block mergers. While size is not a guarantee of efficiency, a number of UK companies compete internationally and even globally in industries where participants perceive great advantage in economies of scale. Thus many industrialists would call for a less restrictive policy in respect of horizontal mergers as a means of encouraging the development of UK-based international champions. The CBI, in its submission to the DTI's recent review of competition policy stated:

The CBI wishes to emphasise the importance business places on the objective of ensuring that the regulatory framework represented by UK competition policy in general and merger policy in particular does not hold back UK based firms in their efforts to compete in global markets.

(CBI, 1987)

While, as Sir Gordon Borrie (1987b) suggests, this aspect may be better dealt with by the MMC following more considered analysis than is possible by the OFT, the fact is that OFT decisions not to recommend the referral of bids to the MMC, where the international dimension is a significant issue, do in effect pre-judge the issue. Moreover, competition criteria based on UK market share have the effect of deterring many potential mergers which may benefit the international competitiveness of British firms.

In contrast to the above arguments, a number of studies, using a variety of yardsticks, have revealed that few mergers are successful in terms of performance after the event (e.g. Singh, 1971; Meeks, 1977; Firth, 1980; Franks and Harris, 1986; Holl and Pickering, 1986). Given the high rate of failure, there is a need, some would argue, for stricter merger controls. Paradoxically, current UK merger policy encourages precisely those mergers which traditionally have had the highest failure rate, i.e. conglomerate mergers. On the other hand, those which have fared best, horizontal mergers, are those which are most likely to be blocked on account of their contravention of the market-share criterion. Finding a solution to satisfy both camps is no easy task.

In the UK, the latest thinking by the Government on merger policy was outlined in the White Paper of January 1988, 'DTI – the Department for Enterprise' (DTI, 1988a). Adherence to the primary criterion of the effect of mergers on competition was reaffirmed. The Government also made a commitment to endeavour to reduce the time taken by the Monopolies and Mergers Commission to consider a merger referral. However, no attempt to restructure the system was indicated. On the other hand, two major changes were proposed which were designed to improve the efficiency of the merger process. First, there will be 'a formal, though non-mandatory, pre-notification procedure'. Second, the Director General of Fair Trading will be empowered 'to obtain undertakings from the parties in cases where it is possible in this way to remove a potential threat to competition without the need for an MMC investigation'. These changes were expected to be incorporated in the next Companies Bill due in December 1988.

SUMMARY AND CONCLUSIONS

Taken overall, merger policy has become more predictable. The controversial disagreements of the early 1980s between the various regulatory authorities have been avoided. However, a number of problems are evident. The resources at the disposal of the Office of Fair Trading are limited to the extent that there is still a strong case for mandatory notification of mergers above a certain size, both before and after deals are concluded. Further, a widely held view, which deserves serious consideration, is that the burden of proof to justify a merger, in the case of *mega-mergers*, should be shifted to the bidder, and that this should involve not only the identification of benefits but also the countering of allegations of potential adverse consequences.

It is also vital that the correct balance is struck between the domestic and the international market in deciding whether to block mergers. A less restrictive policy may be justified taking more sensitive account of the international business context. It is also the case that current merger policy encourages those mergers which tend to have the highest failure rate, the conglomerate mergers, while blocking those most likely to succeed, the horizontal mergers.

3

The Referees: Corporate Conduct and Accountability

The work of organizations involved in the policing of corporate conduct (i.e. the Stock Exchange and the Panel on Takeovers and Mergers) is reviewed in this chapter. The role of the Accounting Standards Committee is also examined, with particular reference to the claims of 'creative' accounting in reporting the effects of takeovers and mergers.

THE STOCK EXCHANGE

Responsibility for the conduct of the stock market rests with the self-regulatory Stock Exchange, which has traditionally controlled its members without any government interference or statutory backing. Under the Financial Services Act 1986, the Stock Exchange is independent of the Securities and Investments Board (SIB) to the extent that it retains its powers in respect of the public issue of securities and Stock Exchange listing. The Act now replaces the Stock Exchange (Listing) Regulations 1984 as a means of implementing the relevant EC Directives. The Stock Exchange is recognized in the Act as the 'competent authority' under the terms of the EC Directives to issue rules governing the terms of admission, listing particulars and continuing obligations, and interim reporting. Thus these requirements governing 'Admission of Securities to Listing' (popularly known as the 'Yellow Book') have statutory backing whereas the remaining rules, which generally impose higher standards, are imposed on the basis of the Stock Exchange's own self-regulatory authority. Given the risk of suspension or withdrawal of listing, irrespective of the nature of the rules, the power of the Stock Exchange is decisive. However, the exercise of powers under the Financial Services Act is subject to the reserve power of the Secretary of State for Trade and Industry to direct the Stock Exchange to comply with the requirements of EC Directives and any other international obligations.

The Securities and Investments Board (SIB), on the other hand, does not have any power to change the rules relating to listing since these are made by the Stock Exchange as the 'competent authority'.

As regards takeovers and mergers, 'listing particulars' are now required for all acquisitions involving the issue of securities, except for issues of shares which would result in less than a 10 per cent increase of shares in a class already listed. Of more significance, however, is Section 6 of the 'Yellow Book' dealing with 'Acquisitions and realizations: takeovers and mergers'. Information is required to be given to the Stock Exchange and in the case of major transactions, circulars sent to shareholders. Approval must be obtained from shareholders for those transactions involving a relationship of 25 per cent or more of the issued equity share capital on the basis of a series of comprehensive tests.

Circulars are required to disclose details of the financial position and profits of the company to be acquired. In the case of 'very substantial acquisitions' or 'reverse takeovers', the acquiring company will normally be treated as a new applicant for listing and subject to additional disclosures, including an accountant's report on the acquiring company itself as well as on the company to be acquired. In such cases, the circular would also be expected to include a pro forma statement combining the information in the two reports and showing the new group's financial position. The circular would also normally include a description of the transaction in broad terms, indicating the nature of the business to be acquired, the value of the consideration and its form, and the likely benefits of the transaction.

The Stock Exchange also prescribes and closely monitors the content of the offer documents relating to takeovers, with the aim of providing shareholders with information essential in assessing the financial merits of the offer. Thus detailed financial information is required in respect of both the bidder and target companies. In addition, the Stock Exchange 'Yellow Book' requires companies to comply with the 'takeover code' of the Panel on Takeovers and Mergers (see next section).

The emphasis of controls by the Stock Exchange is focused on disclosing the financial implications of takeovers for shareholders and protecting shareholder interests. At the same time, given the rate of failure to integrate acquisitions successfully (Porter, 1987), there would seem to be a pressing need for shareholders to be more fully informed about the strategy and industrial logic underlying a takeover in order to provide a longer-term perspective. As David Walker (Chairman of the Securities and Investments Board) has said, in his former capacity as Executive Director of the Bank of England, shareholders should be well informed and 'be able to judge how far a particular bid is likely to bring enhanced efficiency through synergy, or for some other reasons, and how far its attraction rests on the currently highly rated paper of the bidder' (Walker, 1987). It may be that the likely benefits/implications for the economy, the workforce and suppliers could also be outlined in this context, consistent with the earlier discussion on grounds for referral, to explain further and justify takeover proposals.

THE PANEL ON TAKEOVERS AND MERGERS

The Takeover Panel was set up in 1968, on the initiative of the Governor of the Bank of England. The role of this self-regulatory body is to police the conduct of takeover bids, ensuring that all shareholders are treated equally and to see that 'good business standards are observed'. Under the Financial Services Act 1986, the Panel continues as a body independent of the Securities and Investments Board (SIB). However, the SIB has recently brought in measures to support the Panel's work in that advisers in takeover bids will not be permitted to act for clients if there is reason to believe that such clients will fail to comply with *The City Code on Takeovers and Mergers* (Panel on Takeovers and Mergers, 1988a). Moreover, if a person authorized to carry on an investment business fails to comply with the *City Code* or a ruling of the Panel, then authorization by the SIB could be withdrawn. The relationship of the Panel to the SIB, Stock Exchange and other bodies is shown in Figure 3.1.

In recent years the Panel's role as referee has become increasingly difficult. The *City Code* or rule book has been amended and expanded regularly to counteract the growing number of yellow and red card offences by players, some of whom have certainly brought the game into disrepute. Despite this, the Panel has failed to impress some City watchers. In early 1987, for example, former Prime Minister Edward Heath repeated his famous 'unacceptable face of capitalism' phrase to describe corporate conduct during takeover bids.

In response to the Guinness scandal and other problem cases, the Takeover Panel took action to tighten up its rules. In January 1988 a revised *City Code* was issued incorporating a number of changes made during 1987, including an extension of the disclosure responsibilities of intermediaries and the disclosure of details of financing arrangements in the case of highly leveraged bids. The Panel's requirements concerning the disclosure of information about the ownership of companies have been accelerated and extended, i.e. holdings of more than 15 per cent must be disclosed within one business day as must dealings, during formal offers, by those holding 1 per cent or more of the shares of the bidder or

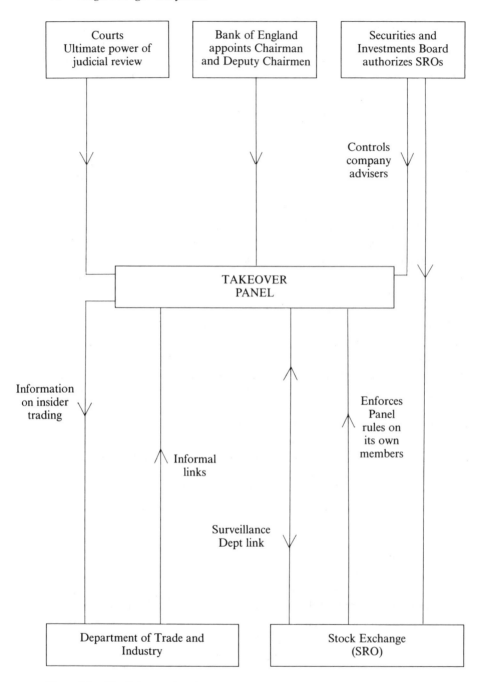

Figure 3.1 *The Takeover Panel and regulation.*

target companies. There remains scope, nevertheless for speeding up the disclosure of initial holdings of 5 per cent or more (currently five days of anonymity is permitted) and for the veil over nominee holdings to be removed. According to the Panel's 1987–88 Annual Report, its revised market surveillance systems are working well. However, it is still probably a little too early to form a considered view of their efficacy under stress.

The Takeover Panel: its role and status

The *City Code* lays down the timetable for bids (see Table 3.1), the documents which must be sent to shareholders and the conditions for making profit forecasts and asset valuations. The Panel regulates the wording of documents issued during takeover bids. Rule 23 requires documents to 'satisfy the highest standards of accuracy and the information contained therein must be adequately and fairly presented'.

The Panel has no legal powers, yet it has been criticized for failing to clamp down on certain practices. Those in favour of its non-statutory status argue that legal powers would only weaken the Panel. They argue that the attraction of its present status is that it allows for speedy, binding rules in takeover battles.

In 1985 the Government had considered whether the Takeover Panel should have statutory backing. This idea was rejected by the Panel itself on the basis that it deals with the whole of industry – not just the City – and that it found the existing arrangements satisfactory. The disadvantage of a statutory system is that this would almost certainly entail a right of appeal against Panel decisions in the courts. Thus, whenever an appeal was lodged it is most likely that the bid would be prolonged. Delaying the bid process could well prove an attractive tactic to the incumbent management of the target firm, but its shareholders may not appreciate this ploy and in any event would have to meet the extra cost of additional legal fees.

On 29 July 1986, a motion put forward by Opposition peers – and supported by Lord Denning, former Master of the Rolls – that the Takeover Panel should be given statutory powers was defeated by 82 votes (161–79) in the House of Lords. During the debates on the Financial Services Act, the Labour Party proposed that the Act was the 'obvious opportunity' to give statutory powers to the Takeover Panel and statutory effect to the *City Code* (Bryan Gould, *The Independent*, 30 January 1987). However, the Government decided not to place the Panel under the umbrella of the Securities and Investments Board because the

Table 3.1   *Summarized timetable of bid procedures*

Event	Timing constraint	City Code/ Companies Act
(1) Approach to target company board		
(2) Preliminary announcement	When any of the circumstances in Rule 2.2 apply	2.2
(3) Firm announcement	Not until offeror is capable of implementing offer	2.5
(4) Post offer document	Within 28 days of (3)	30.1
(5) Target board makes its views known	Within 14 days of (4)	30.2
(6) First closing date	Not earlier than 21 days after (4)	31.1
(7) Announcement of extension (including the statement of expiry date)	Expiry date must be not later than 60 days after (4) (see also Rule 31.5)	31.6 31.5
(8) Announcement of revision	Revised offer to be open for at least 14 days – thus no revision after day 46	32.1
(9) Acceptances may be withdrawn	Not earlier than 21 days after (6), if offer not unconditional as to acceptances	34
(10) Restrictions on target company announcements	After 39th day following (4)	31.9
(11) Announcement that offer unconditional as to acceptances	Not later than 60 days after (4)	31.6
(12) Offer goes unconditional in all respects	Within 21 days of (6) or (11), whichever is later	31.7
(13) Offer closed	Not earlier than 14 days after (11) (see also Rule 33)	31.4 33
(14) (Offer lapses)	On 60th day, if (11) has not occurred, unless (a) Competing offer announced (b) Target board consents to extension (c) Target produces major new information after day 39	31.6 31.9
(15) Consideration posted	Within 28 days after (12)	31.8

Event	Timing constraint	City Code/ Companies Act
(16) 90% acceptances received	Must be within 4 months of (4) to operate compulsory purchase procedures	Companies Act 1985 – ss. 428–30
(17) (Cooling-off period)	If offer lapses, no further offer for 12 months	35.1

Source: Adapted from *Corporate Acquisitions and Mergers* by P.F.C. Begg, 2nd edn 1986, published by Graham & Trotman, London.

Takeover Panel polices the conduct of parties involved in takeover battles that are not members of the SIB.

On the other hand, the Guinness scandal was exposed, it seems fair to assume, because of information that arose from the statutory-based investigation into the affairs of Ivan Boesky. This investigation was the work of the US Securities and Exchange Commission (SEC). Guinness's allegedly illicit dealings were most likely only detected because of the transatlantic inquiries conducted by America's SEC which has statutory powers. Bryan Gould's conclusion was that 'The episode is, therefore, sound evidence for the efficacy of a fully-fledged statutory body with appropriate powers' (*The Independent*, 30 January 1987).

It is also the case that, on at least two occasions in early 1987, the Governor of the Bank of England, Robin Leigh-Pemberton, issued stern warnings to the City to respect the *city code* or face the imposition of 'a more legalistic and consequently less flexible system. The drawbacks of doing so are obvious: we would risk losing the great qualities of speed, commonsense and flexibility that the Panel has been able to display over the years, and which are much admired in other centres. But if that is the price we have to pay for effective enforcement and sanctions, then pay it we shall' (Leigh-Pemberton, 1987).

In the event, the Government decided to maintain the self-regulatory status of the Takeover Panel following measures to tighten up the rules and strengthen the Panel's organizational structure. An interesting development at the EC level, which raises once again the question of statutory controls, is the move by the European Commission to propose a Directive on the conduct of takeovers. While any proposed Directive is unlikely to be inconsistent with the *City Code*, its implementation through UK law would have major implications for the existing non-statutory system.

The structure of the Takeover Panel

The Takeover Panel consists of an Executive which makes the day-to-day decisions, and a 'full panel', which acts as a court of appeal and which, despite its name, does not include the Executive. The Chairman, Deputy Chairmen and Director General (DG) of the Panel are appointed by the Bank of England. The Executive, consisting of the DG, two permanent deputy DGs and a team of six to eight assistant secretaries, take the day-to-day decisions. The 'full panel', led by the Chairman and comprising a dozen representatives of the main City bodies, acts as a court of appeal and thus excludes the Executive, whose original decision is being questioned.

In May 1987 the management structure of the Panel was strengthened on the retiral of then Chairman, Sir Jasper Hollom, and his Deputy, Robin Stormonth-Darling. They were replaced by three people. The new Chairman, Robert Alexander (now Lord Alexander of Weedon), has two deputies, one of whom becomes a director of the SIB. But, as Lord Alexander says, 'Whilst we believe that the service offered by the Panel is generally effective in monitoring the fair conduct of takeovers ... These remain challenging times for all involved in financial regulation, and we shall keep our own standards constantly under review' (Panel on Takeovers and Mergers, 1988b).

THE ACCOUNTING STANDARDS COMMITTEE: ACCOUNTING AND DISCLOSURE STANDARDS

The role of the Accounting Standards Committee (ASC), as a self-regulatory organization established by the professional accountancy bodies, is to make recommendations, in the public interest, on accounting standards for mandatory application by the accountancy profession (e.g. Taylor and Turley, 1986). In the context of takeovers and mergers the relevant standards are the Statements of Standard Accounting Practice (SSAPs) no. 22, *Accounting for Goodwill* (Institute of Chartered Accountants in England and Wales, 1984) and no. 23, *Accounting for Acquisitions and Mergers* (Institute of Chartered Accountants in England and Wales, 1985).

While the terms 'acquisition' and 'merger' are often used synonymously to describe business combinations, in the context of accounting and disclosure standards significant differences arise which impact differentially on profits according to whether 'acquisition' or 'merger' accounting is used. The Confederation of British Industry (CBI) has even gone as far as suggesting, in a consultation paper (CBI, 1987), that a *laissez-faire* accounting atmosphere may have encouraged the boom in takeover and merger activity – by allowing profits after a takeover to be favourably massaged using questionable 'creative' accounting practices permitted by the flexibility of existing accounting standards. While this is a claim that would be difficult to verify, there is no doubt that there is widespread concern and a general belief that something needs to be done. The Department of Trade and Industry (1988b) has echoed this concern in its recent paper *Mergers Policy*, which welcomes the decision by the Accounting Standards Committee to review the relevant accounting standards and to respond to the suggestion that 'There may be too much flexibility in the accounting treatment of mergers and acquisitions and that disclosure is in some cases inadequate to allow the outsider to assess the effects' (p. 11).

Economic and accounting fundamentals

Business combinations can become effective in a variety of ways. A company's assets and liabilities can be purchased directly or indirectly by the purchase of its equity. The structure of the grouping may also be altered, for example through the formation of a holding company to control the existing companies. The consideration involved can also take a variety of forms including equity shares only, cash only or some combination of both.

An important point of principle from an accounting perspective, however, would seem to be that the accounting treatment used to report the effect and substance of a business combination should be independent of the way in which the combination has been achieved. Unfortunately, it does seem to be the case at present under SSAP no. 23, *Accounting for Acquisitions and Mergers* (Institute of Chartered Accountants in England and Wales, 1985) that the choice of 'merger' or 'acquisition' accounting is available more as a consequence of the form of consideration, i.e. equity comprising at least 90 per cent of the fair value, than on the basis of economic or legal criteria which may distinguish a 'merger' from an 'acquisition'.

But is it possible to make an economic distinction in the first place and, if not, then how can differential accounting treatments be justified? The existing accounting rationale suggests that intuitively the term 'acquisition' may be distinguished by using it to describe a business combination where one company dominates or controls the other (see, for example, Taylor, 1987). In this case, there is a holding company which controls a subsidiary company. In company law, there are in fact criteria which establish the existence of a subsidiary. Companies which are not subsidiaries may be associated companies or the result of participation in a joint venture. The term 'merger', on the other hand, is used to describe a business combination which is a confederation or pooling of interests with each company preserving its own identity and autonomy. There are, however, no legal criteria to distinguish a 'merger' from an 'acquisition' though so-called 'merger relief' is available, under conditions specified in the Companies Act 1985, to release the revenue reserves of a subsidiary for distribution to the extent that the form of consideration comprises equity.

But what is the nature of business combinations in practice? In economic terms, there is invariably a dominant managerial strategy and some perception of synergy of operations, finance or administration – indeed these are the motivations underlying the deal. This also applies in a situation where a new holding company is formed to co-ordinate the participating companies. In legal terms, there is invariably a holding company/subsidiary relationship. In effect, there is a transformed or new entity with new economic prospects and new legal relationships. The essence of a business combination is change. As such, it is a distortion to suggest that there are such fundamental differences in the nature of business combinations that different accounting treatments can be justified. Thus the popular use of the term 'merger', as synonymous with 'acquisition' and 'takeover', would appear to be justified. To attempt to differentiate them as accountants do is artificial and inevitably arbitrary.

While a common approach to accounting for 'business combinations' may be justified, it is necessary to understand the major differences between 'acquisition' and 'merger' accounting so that problems concerning the resolution of such differences can be addressed.

Acquisition and merger accounting distinguished

Under acquisition accounting the acquired company contributes to group profits only subsequent to the combination whereas under merger accounting all of the pre-combination profits are included. This in itself provides an artificial incentive to show enhanced profits. Furthermore, under acquisition accounting the investment by the holding company is recorded at market value and the assets and liabilities of the acquired company are revalued to 'fair values' at the date of combination. Under merger accounting the investment is recorded at nominal value and assets and liabilities are not revalued. The effect of this difference is that under the acquisition approach profits subsequent to the combination may be decreased by increased depreciation charges relating to revalued assets. Profits may also be decreased by the amortization of goodwill, though write-offs against reserves are encouraged. Thus there is a further incentive to use merger accounting.

The potential for distorting results does not, however, rest entirely with merger accounting. A pessimistic view of asset revaluations, coupled with provisions for reorganization and anticipated future losses (included in the cost of the purchase), and the immediate write-off of goodwill against reserves may encourage a preference for acquisition accounting.

In the context of conventional accounting principles the rationale for choosing between the two approaches is not well developed, and in fact in SSAP no. 23 *Accounting for Acquisitions and Mergers* it is barely discernible, the only specific criterion being the form of consideration. What this assumes, though, is that the nature of ownership is paramount, irrespective of the economic substance of the business combination.

Accounting practice and regulation: a critique

While merger accounting is currently practised by a small but significant minority of companies in the UK and USA, in many other countries, for example France, West Germany, Italy, Australia and Japan, it is not recognized or permitted (Gray, Campbell and Shaw, 1984; Institute of Chartered Accountants in England and Wales, 1987).

In the UK, the Companies Act 1981, now consolidated in the Companies Act 1985, effectively opened the door to merger accounting by giving limited relief to the requirement to transfer premiums on the issue of shares to a separate, non-distributable share premium account. This so-called 'merger relief' provides that, subject to specified conditions, the required treatment of share premiums does not apply where a company has at least a 90 per cent equity holding in another company. As a consequence of 'merger relief', not only is merger accounting permitted where the necessary criteria are satisfied but a new hybrid form of accounting treatment has emerged, namely where the investment is recorded at nominal value, to the extent that the shares issued by the holding company qualify for merger relief, and acquisition accounting is used in the consolidated financial statements.

Following the Companies Act 1981, SSAP no. 23 (Institute of Chartered Accountants in England and Wales, 1985) was adopted in 1985 defining the conditions under which merger accounting may be used, the accounting treatment of acquisitions and mergers, and the disclosures required for all material business combinations. SSAP no. 23 permits a choice between merger accounting and acquisition accounting if certain conditions are met. These conditions are more restrictive than those legal regulations governing 'merger relief'. In particular, the acquiring company must not hold more than 20 per cent of the equity of the subsidiary prior to the offer, it must have secured at least 90 per cent of the shares, and not less than 90 per cent of the fair value of the total consideration must be in the form of equity. The Seventh EC Directive (1983) on consolidated accounts to be implemented in practice by UK law by 1990 would seem to restrict further these conditions: merger accounting will be permitted only where not more than 10 per cent of the *nominal* value of the total consideration is in the form of cash. There is, however, scope for some variety of interpretation of the precise implications of the Directive and it remains to be seen how it will affect the use of merger accounting in practice. In any event, there is a strong case for eliminating this merger accounting option altogether while permitting 'merger relief' which is designed for a specific purpose, namely to remove the restriction on a holding company from distributing the revenue reserves of a subsidiary in defined circumstances.

While the acquisition approach to accounting for business combinations is widely accepted, there are major problems concerning flexibility and lack of information disclosure. These are not effectively dealt with by SSAP no. 23 and its sister SSAP no. 22 *Accounting for Goodwill* (Institute of Chartered Accountants in England and Wales, 1984). The treatment of goodwill arising on acquisition has been a controversial issue for many years. The Seventh EC Directive (1983) rejected the permanent retention of goodwill as an asset, however, and prescribed useful economic life as a maximum period for amortization. SSAP no. 22 was issued in 1984, rejecting permanent retention, but while preferring immediate write-off of purchased goodwill against reserves it permitted the amortization approach. Furthermore, both treatments are permitted to be used simultaneously as different acquisitions may be accounted for using either method with no justification required. Not only is there a problem of comparability but there is a differential effect on profits depending on the treatment used. This situation can be contrasted with the USA where APB Opinion no. 17 requires amortization over a maximum period of 40 years. Immediate write-off is permitted only if there has been a permanent diminution in value and such write-offs must be charged against profits, not reserves.

If immediate write-off, with the most favourable effect on profits, is chosen then a further problem arises as to the reserves against which the goodwill should be written off. The Seventh EC Directive restricts the use of revaluation reserves for this purpose. Other treatments include capital restructuring, the use of merger reserves and the creation of a 'negative' goodwill reserve. Irrespective of the treatment of reserves there is also the problem that if an acquisition is subsequently sold then the goodwill written off, to the extent that it is recovered, will be recorded, in accordance with current practice, as a gain in the profit and loss account. This asymmetry of treatment distorts reported profits and provides a favourable bias to profits growth.

Given that no recognition is given in accounts to non-purchased goodwill, which is in effect the excess economic value of the business over the value of the individual assets, it is illogical and misleading to retain purchased goodwill as an asset. Unless goodwill can be separately identified as an asset and have an independent market value, which may be the case for a famous brand name for example, then the immediate write-off approach seems the most supportable. So long as the amount of this write-off is fully disclosed, which is not required at present, it seems relatively immaterial how this charge against reserves is presented.

Another major problem area associated with acquisition accounting concerns 'fair value' adjustments (or revaluations) and accounting policy changes. SSAP no. 23 requires the acquiring company to attribute 'fair values' to the individual assets and liabilities acquired. Inevitably, such assessments are subjective. The value of the assets from the acquirer's perspective may well be different from that of the company being acquired. While in some cases assets may be revalued upwards it is also just as likely that values may be reduced, especially in turn-around situations, and the need for reorganization and integration may lead to the creation of provisions for reorganization and associated costs. A particular problem here is that SSAP no. 22 permits provisions for future losses. In addition, there may be differences in accounting policies which will require some adjustments to be made to achieve consistency for the business combination as a whole. While SSAP no. 23 requires information to be disclosed about the impact of accounting policy changes, there are no requirements covering 'fair value' adjustments.

Full disclosure of 'fair value' adjustments seems essential, together with an explanation and justification of the treatment adopted, if users are to form their own judgements of the outcome and merits of a business combination. In particular, disclosure is necessary of both the 'book value' and 'fair value' of the assets and liabilities acquired, including details of provisions. In addition, it would be helpful if explanations were given of significant adjustments from book value whether on account of revaluations or provisions. Another point here concerns the years following the creation of provisions when it is important that any material under-utilization of provisions and subsequent release to the profit and loss account should be disclosed as part of the 'fair value' information.

Accounting and disclosure: the way forward?

Accounting for business combinations is a complex and controversial issue. However, the rationale for 'merger' accounting lacks substance. The situation is also confused by the UK Companies Act 'merger relief' provisions, which apply irrespective of the use of 'merger' or 'acquisition' accounting. Further, SSAP no. 22 *Accounting for Goodwill* and SSAP no. 23 *Accounting for Acquisitions and Mergers* (Institute of Chartered Accountants in England and Wales, 1984, 1985) do not have adequate conceptual and economic foundation. They provide both arbitrary and flexible prescriptions and lack fundamentally important disclosure requirements.

While some proposals for change have been incorporated already in the prior discussion, there is an opportunity at this point to outline a fresh approach to the problem which attempts to reduce both uncertainty and the incentive for manipulation. This approach is based on the premise that it is unrealistic and impracticable to distinguish 'mergers' from 'acquisitions' and that these terms may be used synonymously as in popular parlance. Business combinations invariably involve a transformed or new entity with a dominant managerial strategy and many of the recognized characteristics of an 'acquisition' situation. The accounting consequences of this are that the use of a single method of accounting for business combinations is justified. The most obvious approach would be to base this on the 'acquisition' method, which would recognize the combination as forming a changed entity. Accordingly, only profits subsequent to the combination would be included in group profits. All assets and liabilities of the subsidiary would be reassessed at up-to-date 'fair values'. In respect of the latter point, it would also seem desirable that the assets and liabilities of the holding company and its existing subsidiaries should be reassessed at regular intervals, e.g. at least every five years, so as to ensure some degree of comparability of valuation across the entire group of companies. This approach would also apply in the case of a new holding company being formed to control companies which are party to a combination arrangement.

Full disclosure of the effect of all 'fair value' adjustments and accounting policy changes, together with explanations, would necessarily be required together with any subsequent adjustments to provisions. In this regard, professional guidance would be necessary as to the basis for assessing 'fair values' and the reasonableness of provisions for reorganization and associated costs, including the potential to provide for future losses.

It is also desirable that the treatment of goodwill, arising from the difference between the 'fair value' of the net assets acquired and the market value of the transaction, should be standardized. An immediate write-off to reserves, without exception, is recommended as the most supportable solution. Companies could provide additional information showing the effect of an amortization approach if they so wished. The amounts written off could be disclosed separately in a special 'goodwill reserve' account, thus making clear the nature and impact of adjustments of this kind. Both positive and negative amounts would be transferred to this reserve. Furthermore, subsequent gains or losses on the disposal of assets or subsidiaries should be recognized in the profit and loss account only to the extent that the gain or loss exceeds the goodwill originally transferred to reserves – thus ensuring the symmetrical treatment of gains and losses and removing any incentive for manipulation.

Finally, as a means of becoming more fully informed about the impact of business combinations, it is argued that the contribution of acquisitions to attributable profits and earnings per share should be disclosed in the consolidated accounts when the results of new business combinations are first reported. Major acquisitions should be separately identified then, and also subsequently to the extent that the operations of a subsidiary form identifiable business units. What is suggested here is, in effect, a development of the well-established practice of segment reporting. In this way, overall performance and risk would be subject to finer assessment.

SUMMARY AND CONCLUSIONS

As regards the policing of corporate conduct during the takeover process by the City Panel on Takeovers and Mergers and by the Stock Exchange, the question of whether or not there should be more statutory control remains open to question and is subject to the future performance of the self-regulatory organizations involved.

There is, in any event, a strong case for more in-depth information to be given to investors which will help them to judge better the corporate strategy underlying mergers and the prospects of enhanced efficiency through synergy and other factors. There is also no reason why companies should not be encouraged to report an assessment, in this context, of the effect of a merger on competition and the economy, and to provide firm proposals as to the implications for the workforce, suppliers and other interested parties.

While the Takeover Panel's rules have been tightened up following the experiences of recent takeover battles, there is scope for speedier and more transparent disclosure of shareholdings of any significant stake by a potential bidder.

The issue of accounting and disclosure standards and the role of the Accounting Standards Committee are also deserving of scrutiny. The claim that the flexibility of existing standards provides scope for 'creative' accounting practices appears to be justified. The rationale for the current choice of methods of accounting for business combinations lacks substance. In particular, the user of 'merger' accounting cannot be justified. Furthermore, there is a lack of fundamentally important disclosures. In contrast to current requirements, a single method of accounting for business combinations is proposed based on the 'acquisition' method whereby a new economic entity would be recognized with assets and liabilities assessed at 'fair values'. Full disclosure of all valuations and adjustments would be required as would the contributions of acquisitions to group results. The treatment of 'goodwill' would also be standardized. In this way, not only would investors and other parties have more information with which to appraise new combinations, but there would be greater consistency of treatment across all companies.

The next chapter examines the roles and behaviour of the advisers in the takeover game; these include merchant bankers, advertising agencies, public relations consultants, accountants, solicitors and stockbrokers.

4

The Advisers: Takeover Costs and Tactics

In this chapter, the contribution of external advisers to companies involved in takeover battles is examined, paying particular attention to merchant bankers and corporate communications consultants who, along with most other external advisers, represent the public face of takeovers. Behind the scenes, however, there is sometimes an attempt to use 'dirty tricks' to secure victory with a clandestine world of investigators hired to delve into the personal lives of key figures in the opposing camp, with bribes offered for damaging information. The extent of insider trading is also considered. During a takeover bid, key advisers and/or civil servants may possess share price-sensitive information. Some have succumbed to temptation and abused their position of trust.

Companies recruit a host of advisers in the hope that their takeover team will win the support of the financial institutions (i.e. insurance companies, pension funds, unit trusts). In their annual reports, companies disclose whether any shareholder has a stake of 5 per cent or more. In recent years some foreign firms have acquired significant stakeholdings in several well-known UK firms. Such stakes are often seen as a pre-takeover bid 'stake-out'. For example, General Cinema has had a stake of around 18 per cent in Cadbury Schweppes since 1986. During the Rowntree bid, many observers believed that General Cinema would either mount a full bid, or exploit the chocolate war to sell out at a handsome profit. The Australian food group, Goodman Fielder Wattie held a stake in Ranks Hovis McDougall for some two years before finally mounting a £1.7 bn bid in mid-July 1988 – now withdrawn following referral to the Monopolies and Mergers Commission. Indeed, the 'stake-out' strategy appears popular among predators from the Antipodes in particular.

It is also important to note that, collectively, the financial institutions normally control 70 per cent or more of the equity in Britain's largest firms. These institutions are thus critical in determining the outcome of a takeover bid, and an examination of their policy and role concludes this chapter.

The review of takeover costs and tactics and the issues raised are illustrated by reference to the seven cases of billion pound-plus takeover battles examined in Part II: Elders IXL versus Allied-Lyons, Hanson Trust versus United Biscuits for Imperial, Guinness versus Argyll for Distillers, GEC versus Plessey, Dixons versus Woolworth, BTR versus Pilkington, and Nestlé versus Jacobs Suchard for Rowntree.

TAKEOVER COSTS

Takeover costs in just five of the seven bids examined in subsequent chapters amounted to almost £328 m (see Table 4.1). Fighting a takeover battle is a very costly process, especially for a winning bidder which may not only have to pay a hefty premium and meet its own costs, but also pay the costs of the target firm. Guinness's costs alone in acquiring Distillers amounted to £110 m, or 4.4 per cent of the value of the £2.5 bn takeover. Hanson's costs during its tussle for Imperial were £70 m – more than the post-tax profits in 1985–86 of Dixons, the company which spent £11.7 m in its unsuccessful attempt to woo Woolworth, the latter having spent almost £16 m in its fight to remain independent (see Table 4.1).

Apart from lower costs (it only has to pay its own), the loser in a contested bid (e.g. Argyll, United Biscuits and Suchard) has the opportunity to recoup some of its costs by selling its stake in the target company at a profit, the bid process having pushed up the target's share price. For example, the battle for Imperial cost United Biscuits £21.1 m,

Table 4.1   *Costs incurred in takeover bids*

Bidder	Cost (£ m)	Target	Cost (£ m)
Elders	30.0	Allied-Lyons	14.3
Argyll	48.0	Distillers	–
Guinness	110.0	Distillers	–
GEC	1.4	Plessey	7.5
United Biscuits	21.1	Imperial	–
Hanson Trust	70.0	Imperial	–
Dixons	11.7	Woolworth	16.0
BTR	n/a	Pilkington	9.4
Nestlé	n/a	Rowntree	n/a
Suchard	n/a	Rowntree	n/a

Source: Annual reports.

but after selling its stake, net costs were reduced to just £4.9 m. Argyll was not so fortunate. Despite a £13.9 m profit on its Distillers shares, its net costs were still £34 m. In selling its 29.9 per cent stake in Rowntree, Jacobs Suchard's gross profit amounted to more than £200 m – more than its trading profit of £157 m in 1987.

In an unsuccessful bid, the target company will have spent millions of pounds in fighting off a takeover, but the cost of retaining independence may be dwarfed by the rise in the company's worth due to the attempted takeover. For example, the share price of Allied-Lyons and Pilkington achieved a considerable boost during and after the hostile bids from Elders and BTR, respectively.

There can be little doubt that takeovers have generated business for a number of services. Merchant banks, accountants, advertising agencies, design consultants, financial communications consultants, public relations firms, solicitors, stockbrokers and even private investigators are all in heavy demand during takeover battles. Our review of the role of external advisers begins by examining the linchpin of the corporate advisers – the merchant banks.

THE MERCHANT BANKS

Between 1984 and 1986 the profits of the leading merchant banks with special expertise in corporate finance increased substantially. This was due in no short measure to the underwriting commissions and advisory fees derived from takeovers.

Takeover underwriting first became popular with the cash alternative and is now a regular feature in large bids. It entails the underwriter agreeing to provide target company shareholders with cash in exchange for shares in the bidding company. The risk is that the value of the acquirer's shares may fall, so the underwriters' reward is the payment based on set percentages of the amount underwritten. Payment has conventionally been split three ways. The lead underwriter, the merchant bank, receives 0.5 per cent, the brokers 0.25 per cent, and the sub-underwriters, the investment institutions, receive a 0.5 per cent 'commitment' fee for the first 30 days (plus 0.125 per cent for each subsequent week) and a 0.75 per cent acceptance payment when the offer is complete.

In a bull market the underwriters enjoy two benefits. The risks involved are reduced, while the value of a bid rises. Thus, the underwriting merchant bank is virtually assured of rising profits. In a bear market the reverse applies.

In recent times, the only 'concession' offered by the top merchant banks has been to agree to a reduced rate if the bid fails, but a higher rate if it succeeds. The introduction of success-geared fees has major implications for potential bidders. Companies which can negotiate a reduced commission with their merchant bank in the event of an unsuccessful bid, will be more willing to pursue larger firms, because although the bid value will be great, the penalty for failure to gain control will be reduced. It is unlikely that Argyll would have contemplated bidding for Distillers had Samuel Montagu, its merchant bank, not taken the unprecedented step (for any bank) of agreeing to accept a reduced fee in the event of an unsuccessful bid.

The merchant banks' second source of income from takeovers is advisory fees. Samuel Montagu received no less than £0.5 m in advisory fees for its advisory role to Argyll. As with underwriting commission, these are calculated as a percentage of the value of the deal; 0.5 per cent is the going rate for a medium-sized deal. Smaller bids use the same resources so the fee rises to 1 per cent. Alternatively the banks charge a nominal fee for advisory services in the largest bids where their underwriting commission already assures them of a satisfactory return.

Both underwriting commissions and advisory fees are calculated as a set percentage of the value of a deal, so that the dramatic increase in bid values boosted profits until the stock-market crash. The three largest merchant banks' profits from 1984 to 1987 are shown in Table 4.2. No fewer than fifteen merchant banks acted for at least one client in the seven cases of billion pound-plus deals examined in this book. Morgan Grenfell acted for three bidders (Guinness, United Biscuits and BTR), while Goldman Sachs defended four target companies (Imperial Group, Pilkington, Woolworth and Rowntree) (see Table 4.3).

In 1987, Morgan Grenfell, for the sixth year running, ranked first among financial advisers in respect of UK public takeovers. It acted in 33 transactions worth over £5.3 bn. During this year there were two distinct pauses in takeover activity, caused by the June General Election and October stock-market crash. Despite these temporary breaks in takeover

Table 4.2   *Merchant banks – the profits record*

	1984	1985	1986	1987	
Kleinwort Benson	£44.5 m	£60.3 m	£78.8 m	£64.3 m	(pre-tax)
Morgan Grenfell	£38.8 m	£68.8 m	£82.2 m	£60.8 m	(pre-tax)
S.G. Warburg	£18.2 m	£24.9 m	£41.4 m	£67.1 m	(post-tax)

Source: Kleinwort Benson, Morgan Grenfell, S.G. Warburg.

Table 4.3 *Merchant banks in seven mega-merger battles*

Target	Adviser(s)	Bidder	Adviser(s)
Allied-Lyons	Warburgs/ Shearson Lehman	Elders IXL	Hill Samuel
Distillers	Kleinwort Benson/Fleming	Argyll	Montagu/Charterhouse/ Noble Grossart
Distillers	(as above)	Guinness	Morgan Grenfell/British Linen Bank
Plessey	Kleinwort Benson	GEC	Warburgs
Imperial	Hambros/ Goldman Sachs	Hanson Trust	Rothschilds/Schroders
Imperial	(as above)	United Biscuits	Morgan Grenfell
Woolworth	Rothschilds/ Charterhouse/ Goldman Sachs	Dixons	Warburgs
Pilkington	Schroders/ Goldman Sachs	BTR	Morgan Grenfell
Rowntree	Schroders/ Goldman Sachs	Nestlé	Country Natwest
Rowntree	(as above)	Suchard	Warburgs

Source: Acquisitions Monthly.

activity, Morgan advised 62 clients involved in 97 mergers and acquisitions worth £7.3 bn. In 1985 and 1986, it was involved in 192 takeovers worth almost £22 bn. 1986 was a particularly favourable year: with such levels of activity, Morgan was able to report a pre-tax profit of £82.2 m. 1987, on the other hand, was 'by no means an easy one', as Sir Peter Casey, Chairman, explained in the bank's 1987 annual report. Profits were down more than 25 per cent to £60.8 m. This decline was due principally to the effect of 'Black Monday'.

Apart from being the peak profit year at Morgan, 1986 also represents the peak year in terms of its directors' salaries. In 1986, the average salary of a Morgan director was £157,000, almost double the £82,000 of 1984, but in 1987 the figure slipped to £134,000. Similarly, the highest paid director in 1987 earned £246,639, almost £65,000 less than in 1986.

Prior to 1987, Morgan Grenfell's success was due largely to Roger Seelig (not forgetting the contribution of George Magan), whose ingenuity earned him the nickname 'Roger the Dodger'. Seelig was one of three senior Morgan officials forced to resign in the wake of the Guinness scandal, the others being Christopher Reeves, Chief Executive, and Graham Walsh, head of corporate finance and a former Director-General of the Takeover Panel.

Concern had been aroused by some of Morgan's tactics prior to 'Guinness-gate'. For example, the bank spent £540 m on shares in target companies on behalf of its clients United Biscuits, Guinness and Rank Organization, the latter having bid for Granada. Morgan's purchases were remarkable given the bank's last declared net worth of just £174 m – one-third of the value of its share purchases! The Bank of England intervened to preclude a recurrence of such financial imprudence, by imposing tougher rules to limit a bank's vulnerability to any one company.

The Stock Exchange also had to redraft its rules as a result of share purchases by Morgan for United Biscuits. It had a rule demanding that companies spending 25 per cent of net worth on an investment must consult shareholders beforehand. United Biscuits, with a net worth of just £410 m, had indemnified Morgan for any losses on shares worth £360 m. Indemnity agreements had not been covered by the original rule, so the Exchange had to revise its regulations. As the *Financial Times* concluded, 'If anybody can lay claim to the honour – dubious in many of its competitors' eyes – of having imported US-style aggression to the UK takeover market, it is Morgan' (3 July 1986).

Apart from British merchant banks, a number of US finance houses (e.g. the dual national Crédit Suisse First Boston (CSFB), Goldman Sachs, Merrill Lynch and Morgan Stanley) have made their mark in the City. Goldman Sachs in particular, under John Thornton, has been very successful in winning business from target companies. For example, among others it defended the following companies: Dunlop, Thomas Tilling, Pilkington (all from BTR), Woolworth and Imperial Group. Sachs' reputation as a defence specialist will have been boosted by its recent successes with Woolworth and Pilkington. However, successfully defending target companies must become more difficult as premiums increase. Hence, once Rowntree's value doubled in a matter of weeks, Thornton and his team could do little to save the York-based firm from Nestlé.

Merchant banks now operate in an increasingly competitive international market, and they have gone knocking on corporate doors to win more clients. They have also devised 'special offers' which enable more companies to mount mega-mergers. For example, they have pioneered new financial arrangements which allow firms to secure loans exceeding their own value. Thus, comparatively small concerns can bid for the giants which had before always been beyond their reach. For example, in the summer of 1988, Goodman Fielder Wattie (GFW), the largest Australasian food group, required credit lines of A\$3 bn to finance its £1.7 bn bid for Ranks Hovis McDougall (RHM). This bid has now been withdrawn following referral to the Monopolies and Mergers Commission. One of the major merchant banks responsible for arranging these loans, Samuel Montagu, was a subsidiary of the Midland Bank which had a small proportion of RHM's business. RHM decided to sever all links with the Midland because of the role played by Montagu in financing GFW's bid.

Merchant banks are the 'agents provocateurs' of the takeover game. Their fee assessment policy tends to encourage firms to stretch themselves. This may be in the interests of the banks and their highly paid executives, but it is questionable whether this financial 'happy hour' is always in the client company's best interests.

THE ACCOUNTANTS

Accountancy firms have been involved traditionally in the audit of annual accounts and in providing expert reports on prospectuses and corporate profit forecasts, the latter often forming an important element in a takeover defence strategy. More recently, however, they have expanded their services into the field of corporate finance and have encroached into territory hitherto the sole preserve of merchant bankers. Coopers and Lybrand, for example, was the principal adviser in 124 corporate finance deals in 1987–88 (*Financial Times*, 25 July 1988). Deloitte Haskins & Sells, Ernst & Whinney and Touche Ross are also among the more aggressive players in the market. In the context of takeovers, Deloitte Haskins & Sells became the first accountancy firm ever to appear in the *Acquisitions Monthly* top 20 league table of financial advisers. Ranked at no. 18 for the first half of 1988, the firm was involved in two defences with a total value of £49 m. Starting small, the share issue and merger deals are now getting larger and larger. On the other hand, Peat Marwick McLintock is an example of the more cautious participant, gathering and reporting on financial data and providing back-up to merchant banking advisers.

Accountants are also becoming increasingly involved in hostile takeover bids, not just as part of the back-up team for the merchant banks, but in commenting publicly on the accounts of one or other side in the takeover battle. Coopers and Lybrand's role in defending Pilkington against BTR is the most noteworthy example. Sir Owen

Green, Chairman of BTR, made a complaint to the Institute of Chartered Accountants in England and Wales about Coopers and Lybrand's attack on BTR's profits and cash flow record. However, the Institute's disciplinary committee did not uphold the complaint.

The question of a conflict of interest has been raised where accountants are acting as financial advisers, on the one hand, and reporting accountants and auditors on the other. Some firms, including Peat Marwick McLintock, believe that independence is threatened by attempting to compete with the merchant banks.

FINANCIAL PUBLIC RELATIONS

The financial public relations industry in Britain has its equivalents of Morgan Grenfell and Warburgs in merchant banking. One such firm is Dewe Rogerson. Not only has it acted in every one of the seven takeover battles examined in the following chapters (except for GEC's bid for Plessey, in which GEC relied entirely on its own in-house PR), but it has been on the winning side on each occasion. Table 4.4 shows the public relations advisers involved in the seven mega-bids examined in Part II.

During a takeover bid, the public relations adviser gathers economic intelligence. The adviser is responsible for ensuring that the desired message reaches the proper recipient on time, and for identifying which information should be used to enhance the standing of the client company and dent that of the opposition.

Table 4.4 *Public relations advisers and **contested** mega-merger bids*

Target	PR adviser	Bidder	PR adviser
Allied-Lyons	Charles Barker	Elders	Dewe Rogerson
Distillers	Binns Cornwall	Argyll	Broad Street
Distillers	Binns Cornwall	Guinness	Dewe Rogerson
Plessey	Charles Barker	GEC	In-house PR
Imperial	Hill & Knowlton	Hanson Trust	Dewe Rogerson
Woolworth	Dewe Rogerson	Dixons	Shandwick Consultants
Pilkington	Dewe Rogerson	BTR	Shandwick Consultants
Rowntree	Citigate Communications	Nestlé	Dewe Rogerson
Rowntree	Citigate Communications	Suchard	Shandwick Consultants

Source: Acquisitions Monthly; merchant banks.

Anyone reading the literature which has accompanied the mega-mergers could be excused for holding the protagonist companies and their management in very low regard. Figure 4.1 provides some examples of the costly war of words in takeover battles. This 'war of words' feature excludes the Rowntree bid, because unlike the other bids, Nestlé and Suchard wished to win over rather than alienate Rowntree management. At the same time, the management of the York-based firm no doubt realized that the battle for independence was lost long before the outcome was settled. It too, therefore, had little to gain by delivering a verbal mauling to either bidder.

More importantly, the attempts by Nestlé and Suchard to woo the Rowntree management are perhaps indicative of a growing change in the nature of merger activity. In the past, companies with poor management became takeover targets. In the late 1980s, it is well-managed firms which attract bids. Consequently, there is likely to be a flurry of UK takeover activity in those sectors where British companies are strongest. For example, in food and drinks Ranks Hovis McDougall recently attracted a £1.7 bn bid, now withdrawn, from Australia's Goodman Fielder Wattie, and other Australian entrepreneurs have holdings in Allied-Lyons and Scottish and Newcastle, the latter attracting a bid of £1.6 bn from Elders IXL in October 1988. Cadbury Schweppes and United Biscuits continue to attract the interest of US corporations.

An example of a PR firm at work is Dewe Rogerson's appreciation of the advantages of publicizing a report by Coopers and Lybrand, Pilkington's accountants, which suggested that BTR employed accounting techniques which gave a very favourable impression of its performance. But if a company or its advisers have been haphazard or not absolutely thorough, it is likely that the opposition will take delight in drawing public attention to mistakes or inaccurate information. For example, Dixons criticized Woolworth for failing to capitalize on its large floor space in each store. The Chairman of Dixons, Stanley Kalms, illustrated his point with reference to Woolworth's shop in York. He said that, if successful, he would sell large white goods which would be delivered at the shop rear. This seemed sound enough, until Woolworth's management suggested this might not prove as easy as Kalms imagined. The store backed directly onto the River Ouse.

Not everyone is convinced that public relations firms are important in a takeover battle. According to a spokesman for one major financial institution they are a 'nonsense'. PR firms would obviously dispute that view, and perhaps argue that GEC was mistaken to rely on in-house PR in its unsuccessful bid for Plessey.

Elders of Allied-Lyons
Brands have become tired and have been allowed to flounder.

Leadership and overall strategic direction have been sadly lacking in a group which badly needs both.

Allied-Lyons of Elders
Elders is quite unsuitable to own Allied-Lyons. Elders is too small. Elders' performance has been poor. Elders is seriously overgeared. Elders' management is poor. Elders has not even been an average investment. Elders has inadequate international experience. Elders is a not very successful Australian conglomerate.

Argyll of Distillers
Distillers' poor financial performance is a reflection of its structure and its management.

... a woeful record of failure in the important home market.

The results are well documented and they are disastrous.

Argyll of Guinness
For Distillers, Guinness has a number of profound disadvantages.

Distillers of Argyll
Argyll's record in Scotch whisky to date has shown a lack of strategic direction, a lack of understanding of brand management, and a lack of commitment to the industry.

Guinness of Argyll
Argyll's management competence ... renders it totally unqualified to manage Distillers' international premium brands.

Plessey of GEC
GEC's performance is unimpressive.

GEC is a conglomerate and, like all conglomerates faces the problem of providing strategic direction for diverse businesses. GEC has yet to solve this problem.

GEC of Plessey
Plessey, without a successful merger in telecommunications, faces an uncertain longer term future. Its UK base is not big enough and is under threat from others entering the market.

Imperial Group of Hanson Trust
We strongly urge you to ignore the Hanson takeover bid. We see no logic in it for you or your company.

... in real terms Hanson Industries' organic profits went backwards between 1980 and 1985.

Figure 4.1 *The war of words.*

United Biscuits of Hanson Trust
    Hanson has been married many times before. And some of its partners have been
    left at home to gather dust. Which isn't surprising when you consider Hanson's
    miserly record for capital investment.

Hanson Trust of Imperial Group
    The Imperial board has now lost all credibility having recommended the reverse
    takeover by United.

    Imperial is still seeking an identity.

    Imperial's investment in the US has failed dismally.

Hanson Trust of United Biscuits
    United Biscuits management would be completely overstretched if it succeeded in
    its bid for Imperial.

    Up to now United has been conservative in finance and acquisitions – its largest
    acquisition to date cost some £50 million – but now it is trying to take over
    Imperial which is nearly $2\frac{1}{2}$ times larger than itself and nearly 50 times larger than
    its biggest acquisition so far.

Dixons of Woolworth Holdings
    There's not a retailer in the whole outfit. (Stanley Kalms)

    Basic retailing principles have not been implemented. Many prime sites have been
    abandoned.

Woolworth Holdings of Dixons
    Nothing they have said convinces us that they have any understanding of the
    differences between our businesses and their chain of small electrical shops.

    If you cut out the hype, their record is not as great as it might seem.

Pilkington Brothers of BTR
    BTR's share price has reflected their limited prospects in the absence of frequent
    acquisitions. It is BTR's pedestrian share price performance over the last 12 months
    that lies behind this misconceived bid, not any commercial or industrial logic.

    ... a conglomerate of businesses with short-term horizons.

BTR of Pilkington Brothers
    The poor record of Pilkington over many years is hardly a background against
    which to pontificate on the course of British industry.

Figure 4.1   *The war of words.*

It is estimated that PR advisers earned £25–30 m from contested
takeovers in 1986, with the battle for Imperial alone netting PR firms
£1 m. PR advisers often offer a complete corporate communications
package, and handle advertising too. Fees from advertising tend to be

considerably more than for PR activities.

Advisers to companies fighting takeover battles are often also highly acquisitive companies themselves. Saatchi and Saatchi, the world's largest advertising agency, has identified sixteen segments in the market for 'know-how' and aims to become a leading player in each. While Saatchi's growth and acquisition strategy has been the subject of widespread scrutiny by the business press, another UK company has unashamedly followed the Saatchi path to become the world's largest independent public relations company. Unlike Saatchi though, Shandwick's Peter Gummer has decided to concentrate on PR. Like many of its clients, Shandwick's acquisitions are designed to achieve product concentration and geographical expansion. For example, Japan's biggest PR company, International Public Relations, was recently acquired for £10 m. Since going public in 1984, Shandwick has made twenty-seven acquisitions (as of July 1988), and all these were agreed takeovers. Like Saatchi, Shandwick is averse to hostile bids. As Gummer explains, 'There is no point in a contested takeover in our sort of business.' As Table 4.4 shows, Shandwick has represented a client in three of the seven cases of billion pound-plus takeover battles examined in subsequent chapters.

TAKEOVER ADVERTISING

Normally the target firm in a hostile bid strikes the first blow and spends the most money in the war of words. For example, before Elders made its formal offer, Allied-Lyons had responded to speculation and began erecting its defences. On Sunday 22 September 1985, the 'quality' newspapers each carried a double-page spread advertisement by Allied-Lyons. At the time, *The Sunday Times* charged £31,000 per page, so this advertisement in this paper alone cost £62,000. According to one estimate, Saatchi and Saatchi's advertising fees amounted to £3 m, while Dewe Rogerson's from Elders were half this amount (*The Sunday Times*, 27 October 1985).

Companies are naturally reluctant to reveal the amounts they spend on advertising during takeover bids, but one can be certain that the amounts quoted above are not exceptional for a mega-merger battle. Fiona McPhail examined corporate advertising in the battle for Distillers. She selected three newspapers – the *Financial Times, The Times* and, because of the Scottish dimension, *The Glasgow Herald.* She calculated expenditure on advertisements in these three newspapers *alone* as follows: Distillers spent an estimated £674,786, Argyll £1,459,531, and Guinness £1,660,446 (McPhail, 1987).

During a takeover bid every advertisement must first be approved by the Takeover Panel. If it refuses to authorize an advertisement, the company affected may have an enforced break in its advertising programme. For example, Allied-Lyons had no press advertisements during the week 2–9 November 1985.

By April 1986, the contested battles for Distillers and Imperial Group had reached the final stages. Throughout these bids, newspapers carried full-page advertisements which more often than not were an attempt to demolish the opposition's credibility. It came as no surprise, therefore, when the Takeover Panel introduced new rules, which came into force on 7 April, to clamp down on 'knocking copy' during a takeover bid.

There have been a few critics of the Panel's clamp-down on advertisements during a takeover bid, but, on the whole, it has been well received. The standing of the Panel (and that of the Advertising Standards Authority) was hardly enhanced when advertisements which the Panel had approved led to legal action. Roddy Dewe of Dewe Rogerson fully supports the restrictions on takeover advertising which the Takeover Panel imposed in April 1986: 'It was very sensible. There was absolutely no control' (interview with Dewe, 19 August 1987). Nevertheless, despite the Takeover Panel's ruling, advertising agencies have remained a key member of any takeover team involved in a mega-merger.

Perceptions of a company are shaped to a large extent by its advertising and PR. Companies must therefore ensure that they have nurtured a positive image, especially in the City and among influential journalists and stockbrokers. Establishing such a rapport once a hostile bid has been received will prove exceptionally difficult, if not impossible. The recent bout of mega-bids appears to have opened executives' eyes to the dangers of a low profile and poor PR. For example, television commercials which once merely promoted brands are now being used to promote the company itself (e.g. adverts for Allied-Lyons, Blue Arrow, Hanson Trust, ICI and Pilkington).

Britain's largest companies may once have been coy about their size and achievements, but now they seem to have adopted a position of 'If you've got it, flaunt it.' This is particularly evident in Allied-Lyons' 'A Great British Company' commercial, which is a clever compilation of clips from the numerous commercials it runs to promote its many brands (e.g. Babycham, Castlemaine XXXX, Tetley's Tea).

While takeover advertising is by its very nature public, the battle for corporate control also involves private, secret activities, in other words 'dirty tricks'.

DIRTY TRICKS

'Dirty tricks' and black propaganda have featured in several takeover battles. It appears that companies will use any and every means to gain victory, even stooping to spying on executives of the rival firm, and bugging the opposition's offices and board room. If economic arguments fail to sway shareholders, perhaps the threat of a scandal may be sufficient to secure victory in the battle for corporate control.

During the takeover battle for Bell's, the Scottish whisky firm, it appeared that either Guinness or its supporters employed individuals to 'muck rake' into the personal lives of Bell's Chairman, Raymond Miquel, and Bill Walker, the Conservative MP whose Perth constituency included Bell's headquarters (*The Money Programme*, BBC TV, 1 February 1987).

When Argyll bid for Distillers, private eyes trailed Argyll chief executive, James Gulliver, and the former Government Minister, Sir Alex Fletcher, MP, an independent adviser to Argyll, had his London flat ransacked and he himself was told to 'back off' by some 'heavies'. At the same time, firms in the Guinness camp were taking precautions against bugging, or 'audio-surveillance' as the private eyes call it. Offices of firms such as Binns Cornwall, the public relations firm, were swept morning and night for listening devices. David Connell (a Distillers director) had papers stolen from his house and various executives believed they were being followed.

In January 1986, Charles Walford, a former Gulliver employee, was approached in New York by a man calling himself Nicholas Vafiadeis of Tempest Consultants, a firm which, according to his business card, carried out international investigations. Walford was offered $10,000 in exchange for any information on Gulliver which would be sufficient to lose him his bid for Distillers (*The Money Programme*, BBC TV, 1 February 1987).

According to Chris Brogan of Security International Ltd, one of the leaders in the field, his company has worked on many takeover bids in the UK, a number of which were large enough to attract considerable interest in the financial press. Security International was employed by one camp during the three-cornered contest between Argyll and Guinness for Distillers. During this bid, the demand soared for the services of those experienced in gathering 'intelligence'. This heavy concentration of London's private investigators had its lighter moments. Two company executives under surveillance were seen to enter a public house which quickly filled as teams of investigators followed suit. Until then, the investigators had been unaware that so many of their profession were working on the case, but in this small bar they literally came face to face with one another (interview with Brogan, 19 August 1987).

Surveillance has been used in other bids too. For example, Dixons has admitted to employing a private detective during its £1.8 bn bid for Woolworth. Inquiries centred on the private lives of Chief Executive, Geoffrey Mulcahy, and director, Nigel Whittaker (*The Observer Business*, 15 February 1987). In addition, the telephone of the buying director of Comet, a Woolworth subsidiary, was illegally tapped. A security consultant engaged by Dixons was accused of paying two men to intercept this director's telephone calls (*Financial Times*, 2 February 1988).

In addition to the array of advisers gathered together by the opposition, a company should not overlook, as recent evidence suggests, the fact that some of its own highly paid advisers may jeopardize the company's plans by 'insider trading'. The next section examines evidence of this illegal activity in the mega-merger battles.

INSIDER TRADING

Prior to launching a bid, and at critical stages during it, a company must maintain strict secrecy. Once the market suspects that either a bid or a higher one is imminent, the share price of the target firm is likely to rise dramatically, and thus its market worth. For example, one month before the Guinness bid, the share price of Bell's stood at 143p, but the day before the bid it had risen to 192p.

Maintaining secrecy has eluded many bidders. An examination of target company share prices immediately before they were subject to a takeover offer suggests that insider trading has reached epidemic proportions. *Acquisitions Monthly* has highlighted the rise in share prices prior to a bid. The rise in the share price of the target companies in the cases examined in this book are shown in Table 4.5. The sharp rise in Rowntree's share value was due to Suchard acquiring a large stake prior to a bid by either itself or Nestlé.

The City of London's reputation has certainly been blemished by the insider trading epidemic. A number of the City's stars have resigned because they had abused their already highly paid positions to boost their income illegally. Civil servants at the OFT may also have exploited a position of trust. Suspicions have been raised by increases in the share prices of target firms immediately prior to government announcements that bids would not be referred to the Monopolies and Mergers Commission. For example, BTR called for an inquiry into the Pilking-

Table 4.5 *Price moves on the London Stock Exchange before the news of a takeover bid*

Company	Price (p)	1 month before	1 day before	Value of bid	Change over month (%)
Allied-Lyons		227	267	255	+12
Distillers[1]		465	510	505	+ 9
Distillers[2]		477	572	604	+27
Imperial[3]		217	240	237	+ 9
Imperial[4]		250	291	332	+33
Plessey		130	136	162	+25
Woolworth		487	633	688	+41
Pilkington		483	530	530	+10
Rowntree		473	752	890	+88

Source: Acquisitions Monthly.

[1] Argyll bid announced 2 December 1985.
[2] Guinness bid announced 20 January 1986.
[3] Hanson bid announced 6 December 1985.
[4] United Biscuits bid announced 17 February 1986.

ton's share price movements in the two days before the Government's announcement. Although the decision not to refer was expected in terms of the Government's commitment to base decisions 'primarily on competition grounds', the political furore surrounding the bid was such that a decision to refer would not have been surprising. As BTR claimed, however, the market seemed certain the bid would not be referred.

The merchant banks, communications consultants and other advisers are all employed by companies determined to win the day. The outcome of a takeover battle is influenced by these bodies, but the final decision whether to accept or reject an offer rests with the financial institutions.

THE FINANCIAL INSTITUTIONS

Financial institutions control more than 70 per cent of the equity capital of British 'blue chip' companies. Their decisions are critical in determining the outcome of takeover battles. Although they were not asked to cast their votes in the Elders vs Allied-Lyons and BTR vs Pilkington bids, a brief examination of their shareholdings in the two target firms confirms their importance, and especially that of the Prudential, by far the largest institutional investor. The Pru' owns 'just under 4 per cent of Great Britain PLC' (Moir, 1986, p. 103).

The Prudential was the largest shareholder in Allied-Lyons, Distillers, Pilkington and Woolworth. It is also the largest shareholder in at least one of the bidding companies featured in Part II. It has a stake of nearly 7 per cent in GEC. Moreover, it also has a stake in at least two of the most successful merchant banks, Kleinwort Benson and Morgan Grenfell. Just before Elders IXL made its bid the Australian company held 40.5 m shares in Allied-Lyons. The six largest institutional shareholders in Allied-Lyons were the Prudential (25.4 m), the Norwich Union (17.6 m), the National Coal Board Pension Funds (14 m), Scottish Widows (11 m), Electricity Council Pensions (10.5 m) and Provident Mutual (9.2 m).

There were eighteen major institutional shareholders in Pilkington when BTR made its bid. Once again, the Prudential was by far the largest shareholder with over 7 m shares, with the Norwich Union the second largest with over 2 m, followed by a group of five which each held between 1 and 2 m shares. The clout of the two largest shareholders was not lost on Pilkington's supporters. As Ken Hind, Conservative MP for West Lancashire said: 'If the Prudential and Norwich stay with us, we will see off this bid. If they sell out the smaller ones will follow' (*Financial Times*, 8 January 1987).

In the Dixons bid for Woolworth, the institutions were called on to support or reject the bid. The Prudential was again the largest investor in the target company, with a stake which varied during the bid from 7.5 to 8 per cent. The institutions rejected Dixons because they were unconvinced that the bidder would improve on the performance of incumbent management. More importantly, in 1982 Woolworth warned the institutions that they would need seven years to achieve their objectives. In 1986, they were ahead of schedule, and the institutions decided that the management at least deserved their backing until 1989, when the seven-year period elapsed. During the first half of 1986, the financial institutions had been accused of 'short-termism', but their decision to continue to back Woolworth's management rather than Dixons did much to refute this allegation.

Many of the largest institutions have a policy rule that they will support the target company in a takeover situation. They will withhold their support, however, if the management has failed to achieve satisfactory returns (e.g. the institutions interviewed cited Distillers as a very badly run company unworthy of future backing), or if the offer price is a clear overvaluation of the target company, even allowing for an average premium, as the institutions have a fiduciary duty to investors.

When mega-merger fever has been at its height, some institutions have used their annual reports to deny that they base their decisions on a short-term perspective. The Prudential, for example, stated: 'Our judgement is not made on short-term considerations.' In fact, the Prudential claims it has a bias in favour of the target company. It has 'a predisposition to support incumbent managements in good standing wishing to remain independent, qualified by the view that at some price a bid can be too attractive for us properly to reject it'.

Apart from economic factors, in weighing up a takeover bid the institutions may also assess the social consequences of a takeover. One of the largest institutions said it would always reject an offer if the consequences of the takeover were 'socially unacceptable'. It singled out leveraged bids as a cause for concern. While it accepted the need for restructuring, the institution explained that the nature of leveraged bids demands sell-offs to recoup the purchase price. Such divestments may lead to plant closures and unemployment, and thus this institution would be unlikely to lend its support to a leveraged bid.

Companies spend considerable time and resources during takeover battles, and this expenditure is warranted because the institutions as a rule wait until the very last minute before deciding whether to back the bidder or the target. However, opinion differs among the institutions on the effectiveness of advertising and other takeover documents issued in the course of the battle. One of the largest institutions reads them very carefully in order to evaluate and question executives and their 'chaperones, the merchant bankers', while another paid scant regard to documents, and dismissed advertisements as 'nonsense'.

The institutions may have a slight bias towards incumbent management, but their final decision rests on the quality of the case presented by the alternative managements and the size of the offer. In the course of the Swiss bids for Rowntree, the institutions decided not to back Rowntree. On the one hand, some professional investors took the view that Rowntree had made insufficient progress, while others – aware of their professional obligations to clients – were understandably enticed by the opportunity to double their money and sell out to one of the Swiss suitors.

With most bids involving offers of shares, the share price of the bidding firms is critical in determining the outcome of a takeover battle. The financial institutions, in the final analysis, tend to respond to a high price, this being the short-term opportunity available, rather than the longer-term promise of improved results from incumbent management. A more proactive role in corporate management, through influencing changes in strategy or the management team, is an alternative not currently contemplated by the financial institutions.

SUMMARY AND CONCLUSIONS

As the number and size of bids have grown, so too has the fee income of the external advisers, whose reputation and revenue are also the outcome of their effectiveness. As in boxing, the men in the corner do very well if they have a successful fighter. The soaring profits and salaries of takeover advisers testify to the takeover boom.

Indeed, the advisers are often paid more than the chairmen and chief executives of their clients, large multinational corporations. For example, Olivier Roux was seconded to Guinness from Bain & Co., the management consultants, shortly after Ernest Saunders became Chief Executive. In 1984, Roux, then 34, was promoted by Saunders to the Guinness board, as Finance Director. Saunders tried to persuade Roux to join Guinness on a permanent basis, but he gave up when he discovered that Roux – 15 years his junior – earned much more than he did, and that this salary, 'if published, would have put Roux among the two or three most highly paid men in Britain' (Fallon and Srodes, 1987, p. 205).

Some may find this situation alarming. The market places a higher value on the services of comparatively youthful, but no doubt highly talented, management consultants/merchant bankers, than on the 'captains of industry', who are responsible for wealth creation and whose decisions determine the prosperity of the company itself, its shareholders and its employees. Unless the differential in rewards narrows, industry may fail to attract and retain managers capable of emulating the business achievements of men like Sir Owen Green, Lord Hanson, James Gulliver and Sir Hector Laing.

To the financial institutions too, it tends to be the short-term financial rewards from rocketing share prices in a takeover bid which determine their behaviour – which may be rational, given their passive stance to their investments, but not necessarily beneficial to Britain if a foreign takeover results. The costs of takeovers are also enormous and it may be that a more interventionist approach by the institutions could do much to remedy the weaknesses in management that are exposed by a bid and possibly prevent unnecessary takeovers where the aim of the predator is to enhance market power.

Some economic historians have blamed Britain's industrial decline on social attitudes which have held finance in relatively high esteem compared to industry, which was regarded as somewhat vulgar and ungentlemanly. It appears that these values persist, even despite efforts to promote the enterprise culture.

Seven case studies of billion pound-plus bids now follow. The takeover battles are examined in the chronological order in which each bid was launched, starting with Britain's largest ever bid at the time – the Australian brewer Elders IXL offering £1.8 bn for Allied-Lyons. Not long afterwards, this record was broken twice in the same week. On 2 December 1985 Argyll set a new record with its £1.9 bn bid for Distillers, and on the same day United Biscuits agreed to join Imperial Group in a £1.3 bn merger. The following day, GEC launched its £1.2 bn bid for Plessey. Four days after Imperial had agreed a friendly merger with United Biscuits, it received a hostile £1.9 bn bid from Hanson Trust.

Shortly after the exciting denouement to the Distillers and Imperial contests, Dixons launched its bid for Woolworth, but already the takeover climate had changed. The Takeover Panel had prohibited 'knocking copy'. Woolworth, advised by Goldman Sachs, successfully fought off Dixons, and by the year end Sachs' services were once again in demand. It advised Pilkington in its defence against BTR, the acquisitive conglomerate. This was the first mega-bid following the Guinness scandal, and in retrospect BTR could not have mounted its bid at a less opportune moment.

While the City recovered from 'Guinness-gate', UK companies increasingly turned to the USA for acquisitions. By spring 1988, even Guinness itself was once again making acquisitions, if not in the UK. The time was ripe for a major deal, and it came when Nestlé weighed in with a £2.1 bn bid for Rowntree.

PART II

TAKEOVER BATTLES

5

Elders IXL Versus Allied-Lyons

INTRODUCTION

Both Allied-Lyons, the British food and drinks giant, and Elders IXL, the Australian conglomerate, have diversified and grown through acquisitions. In the autumn of 1985, Elders made a bid for Allied-Lyons, a company four times its size in terms of market value.

The first public indication that Elders was interested in acquiring Allied-Lyons was given on 5 September 1985. On 21 October 1985 it unveiled its cash offer for Allied-Lyons. At £1.8 bn, the bid was almost double the previous British record set in 1983 when BAT Industries paid £960 m for the insurance group, Eagle Star. The bid was unique because of its size, and never before had a leveraged bid of such magnitude been made in the UK. The debt-financed nature of the bid aroused concern at the Office of Fair Trading (OFT), and on its advice, Leon Brittan, the Minister, referred the bid to the Monopolies and Mergers Commission (MMC) in early December. This investigation by the MMC was thus seen as a test case for highly leveraged bids in Britain.

The decision to refer the bid underlined the fact that UK merger policy was at the time not based *exclusively* on competition grounds. The MMC was unable to conclude its investigation within six months, and it received a three-month extension from the Minister. In September 1986, despite the Bank of England's opposition, the MMC decided that the bid was not against the public interest.

Shortly afterwards, Elders achieved the main objective underlying its bid for Allied-Lyons: the acquisition of market access for its brewing operations. It gained access to 'the beerage' by acquiring Courage brewery from Hanson Trust for £1.4 bn. Allied-Lyons was now superfluous to Elders' plans.

THE COMPANIES COMPARED

Allied-Lyons

In 1961 three breweries merged to form Allied Breweries, and in 1968 Showerings, famous for its Babycham drink, was acquired. In 1975, Sir Keith Showering became Chairman, and three years later he master-minded the merger with J. Lyons, the food company.

Allied-Lyons is one of Britain's leading food and drink companies with a stable of well-known brands (see Table 5.1). In 1985, it had a market capitalization of £1.92 bn, four times that of Elders (see Table 5.1). On the basis of sales, it ranked as the 21st largest company in the United Kingdom – Elders would not even have been included in the top 100. In 1985 Allied-Lyons consisted (as it still does) of three divisions: beer, wines

Table 5.1   *The companies compared*

	Elders IXL*	Allied-Lyons†
Sales	A$7.00 bn	£3.17 bn
Pre-tax profits	A$133.45 m	£219 m
Number of employees	21,000	44,967
Main interests	Brewing: Foster's Lager. Pastoral activities: woolbroking, livestock selling, international processing and trading. Financial: merchant banking, property finance, retail finance.	Brewing: Double Diamond, Skol, Ind Coope, Long Life. Wines, spirits, drinks: Coates Cider, Britvic fruit juices, Teachers' whisky, Harvey's sherries, tea, coffee, cakes and ice cream.

Source: Annual reports.
*Year to June 1985.
†Year to March 1985.

Table 5.2   *Allied-Lyons: divisional turnover and profits*

Division	Turnover (£ m)		Profits before tax (£ m)	
	1986–87	1985–86	1986–87	1985–86
Beer	1,539.3	1,333.5	157.5	118.3
Wines and spirits	870.5	849.3	113.9	80.1
Food	1,249.4	1,205.2	88.5	74.5

Source: Allied-Lyons (1987) Annual report.

and spirits, and food. The relative turnover and profits of these divisions are given in Table 5.2. In 1985–86, all three divisions were profitable but while the food division had a far higher turnover than the wines and spirits division, it contributed less to the group's profits (see Table 5.2).

Elders planned to keep the two drinks divisions of Allied-Lyons, but sell the food division, 'as it had no logical fit' with either Allied-Lyons' other two divisions, or with the combined Elders–Allied-Lyons group.

Elders

Elders IXL is an Australian brewing, farming and finance group, best known in Britain for its Foster's Lager. It is comprised of four core businesses – the Elders Carlton Group, Elders Pastoral Group, Elders International Group and Elders Finance Group – with a total of 21,000

Table 5.3   *Elders IXL: principal acquisitions since formation in 1981*

Date	Company	Principal area of business	Cost	Activity
1982	Wood Hall Trust	Australia	A$115 m	Pastoral
1982	Bridge Oil	Australia	A$54 m	Oil
1983	Westwools	Australia	A$16 m	Wool
1983	F. J. Walker	Australia	A$23 m	Meat
1983	Mayfair Foods Ltd (50%)	Australia	A$14 m	Meat
1983	Carlton and Utd Breweries	Australia	A$998 m	Brewing
1983	Kidston Gold Mining (20%)	Australia	A$25 m	Mining
1984	Goodman Group (20%)	New Zealand	A$67 m	Conglomerate
1984	Roach Tiley Grice (40%)	Australia	Not disclosed	Stockbroking
1984	PICA	Asia	US$20 m (A$29 m)	Banking
1985	Yates Corp.	New Zealand	A$34 m	Pastoral
1985	Repco automotive business	Australia	Not disclosed	Automotive

Source: Allied-Lyons press release, 'IXL – briefing for the Press', 7 November 1985.

employees (including full- and part-time staff). In the year ended 30 June 1985, its turnover was little less than A$7.0 bn, making it Australia's second largest quoted group in terms of turnover. Its market capitalization was A$900 m (£452 m), ranking it as the 15th largest company in its home country. Prior to bidding for Allied-Lyons, Elders had made many acquisitions, but the most significant was the A$998 m purchase in 1983 of Carlton and United Breweries, Australia's largest brewer (see Table 5.3).

In 1983 the six main UK brewers accounted for about 75 per cent of the 37.8 m bulk barrels sold in Britain in 1982. They owned half the country's 76,000 public houses and accounted for more than 80 per cent of lager volume sales (*Financial Times*, 18 March 1987). By 1985 Elders had decided to establish itself as one of Britain's largest brewers, and was examining possible takeover targets. It chose Allied-Lyons, Britain's second largest brewer (see Table 5.4).

Table 5.4   *The state of the beerage*

	Brand	Market share (%)	No. of pubs
Bass	Carling Black Label Tennent's	20	7,400
Allied-Lyons	Skol Long Life Castlemaine XXXX	13	6,800
Watneys	Foster's Carlsberg Budweiser	13	6,400
Whitbread	Heineken Stella Artois	12	6,600
Scottish & Newcastle	Harp McEwan's Kestrel	10	1,450
Courage	Hofmeister Harp Kronenberg	8.5–9	5,000

Source: The Sunday Times, 21 September 1986.

THE BATTLE

The preparations

In February 1985, Elders took the first step towards acquiring Allied-Lyons. On 22 February 1985, Windemere Securities Ltd, later an associate of Elders, began to buy the first of the 40.7 m shares (a stake of 6 per cent) it held in the British company on the day the bid was launched. It paid 176p for the first shares.

By August, the press were speculating that Elders would bid for Allied-Lyons. On 23 August, Sir Derrick Holden-Brown, Chairman of Allied-Lyons, wrote to his opposite number in Elders, Sir Ian McLellan (who retired in November 1985), seeking clarification of Elders' intentions. Almost a fortnight later, Elders responded to Sir Derrick's letter, saying that a group of international banks, co-ordinated by Citibank, was close to finalizing conditional loan commitments which would permit Elders to fund an offer of 250p per share for the whole of the issued ordinary share capital of Allied-Lyons. The statement said: 'It is too early to state whether any offer will be made but such offer, if made, will not be less than 250p per Allied-Lyons ordinary share. Elders expects to be in a position to clarify the situation within six weeks.'

As the six-week deadline drew near, Elders had not yet clarified its position. The Takeover Panel intervened to remind the Australian company of its promise to clarify its position. It instructed Elders to issue a statement by 21 October, indicating whether or not it intended bidding for Allied-Lyons.

The bid

On 21 October 1985, a £1.8 bn cash bid (255p per share) was launched. At the time, this was by far the largest ever bid for a UK company. It was also the first major leveraged bid for a UK company.

Strictly speaking, IXL – not Elders IXL – was the bidder. IXL was an unlimited British company, incorporated specifically to act as a bidder. Its complicated ownership structure was unusual, to say the least. After a week-long investigation, Allied-Lyons issued a statement 'IXL – briefing for the Press' which said that 'Citibank and other banks are apparently contemplating a course of action which in the present circumstances of Allied-Lyons is illegal'. Elders complained to the Takeover Panel, and the following day Allied-Lyons was forced to withdraw its accusation.

Although there were no competition grounds for referring the bid to the MMC, Leon Brittan, the Secretary of State for Trade and Industry, heeded the advice of the Director General of the OFT, and referred the case to the MMC. This was the first takeover bid referred to the MMC on grounds other than competition since Norman Tebbit's speech of July 1984 in which he stated that cases would be referred primarily on competition grounds. The Elders' bid automatically lapsed as a result of the referral.

On 12 March 1986, Elders sold its entire 6 per cent stake in Allied for £125 m or 306p per share, making a profit of around £41 m. Even allowing for its costs incurred in the bid, this still left a profit of £11 m. According to John Elliot, the sale was a tactical move rather than a strategic withdrawal. In the meantime, the MMC investigation continued, and Elders was asked to supply detailed financial information on its bid for Allied-Lyons. On 24 March 1986, Elders lodged an application for judicial review of the proposal made by Sir Godfray Le Quesne, Chairman of the MMC at the time, that disclosure was necessary on grounds of natural justice and for the Commission to fulfil its statutory duty. This view was not shared by Elders which said that giving Allied this information three or more months before it would be in a position to launch a renewed bid, would seriously prejudice its ability to mount an offer. Elders said that Sir Godfray planned to give Allied-Lyons a copy of its submissions to him on its future financing plans and bid tactics.

Elders was given leave by the High Court to challenge the legality of the MMC's proposal, but the High Court dismissed Elders' plea for an order quashing the decision of the MMC to disclose information to Allied-Lyons. Meanwhile, Allied-Lyons agreed to pay C$2.6 bn (£1.25 bn) for the spirits and wines division of Canada's Hiram Walker Resources. Hiram's brands include, among whiskies, Canadian Club and Ballantynes, plus Courvoisier cognac and the liqueur Tia Maria.

This deal was interpreted as a defensive measure on the part of both companies, as each was the target in a hostile bid. By selling its drinks division, Hiram hoped that its predator, Gulf-Canada, would abandon its bid. Similarly, at the time, once this purchase was complete, Allied-Lyons hoped to have placed itself beyond Elders' price range. But this mutually beneficial arrangement failed to stop Gulf-Canada Corporation from acquiring Hiram. Olympia and York Enterprises Ltd, Gulf-Canada's parent company, challenged the Hiram–Allied-Lyons contract in the Canadian courts.

After months of uncertainty and legal proceedings, in a joint press release of 5 September 1986, Allied-Lyons and Gulf-Canada announced that they had reached agreement over the future ownership and management of Hiram Walker Spirits. Hiram Walker Spirits would be operated as a joint venture with Allied-Lyons having a 51 per cent stake. It would be wrong to present the Hiram acquisition as simply a defensive move. After all, the main strategy of the wines and spirits division is the development of its international brands and world markets. The acquisition of Hiram Walker Spirits achieved in one step what would otherwise have taken a number of years.

The MMC decision

During its investigation, the MMC had received submissions from a number of parties overtly opposed to the bid, while the Department of Trade and Industry and the Scottish Office merely expressed their concerns. Critics included the Bank of England, a number of trades unions (though the Transport and General Workers' Union (TGWU), representing 'over 20 per cent' of the Allied-Lyons workforce, neither opposed nor supported the bid), the Campaign for Real Ale, various trade organizations, rival companies, including Bass, and suppliers and customers.

Despite this array of opposition, the MMC unanimously decided that Elders should be allowed to bid for Allied-Lyons. On 3 September, the Secretary of State announced that the bid could proceed. Allied-Lyons shares fell 6p on the day to close at 347p – virtually double their value of 18 months earlier when Elders began acquiring a stake in the company. The market capitalization of Allied-Lyons was £2.34 bn, and the Hiram acquisition had yet to be finalized.

When the case had been referred in December to the MMC, Elders' bid had automatically lapsed. Under Rule 35 of the Takeover Panel's rules, the Australian company now had three weeks (i.e. until 24 September) to launch a new bid. Otherwise it had to wait until the anniversary of when its offer had lapsed (i.e. early December). Shortly before this deadline expired, Elders paid Hanson Trust £1.4 bn for the Courage brewery and pubs. It had gained access to 'the beerage'. Acquiring a UK brewer had been the prime motive behind the Allied-Lyons bid. This objective had been achieved and Elders did not renew its bid. Allied-Lyons had won its year-long battle for independence.

THE AFTERMATH

Since the Elders bid, Allied-Lyons has succeeded in reporting impressive results which have often exceeded the City's expectations. Turnover has grown by 27.3 per cent since 1986, from £3.3 bn to £4.2 bn in 1988, and profits have increased by 62 per cent from £269.5 m to £436 m. Despite this solid performance, Allied-Lyons remains a likely takeover target. This time the predator may again come from Australia. Alan Bond's Bond Corporation is currently the company's largest shareholder. The Australian tycoon is clearly intent on consolidating his company's position as one of the largest players in the brewing industry. This sector is likely to become increasingly popular as style-conscious drinkers pay hefty premiums for imported beers. Hence in the USA, many drinkers shun American products such as Budweiser and prefer the more expensive, Dutch beer, Heineken. In Europe, too, many consumers prefer beers of other countries, and in the UK, Australian beers brewed under licence from Elders and Bond have proved especially popular.

Significantly, the beer division of Allied-Lyons is emerging as the star performer of the company, and its present head, Richard Martin, has been chosen to succeed Sir Derrick Holden-Brown as the group Chief Executive from January 1989. Whether Allied will remain independent for much longer is problematic. The company faces a major dilemma. The food and drink sector is becoming increasingly concentrated globally. In order to remain internationally competitive, another major acquisition may be necessary. On the other hand, a large deal would dilute earnings in the short term, thus rendering Allied's share price vulnerable and the company liable to takeover once again.

One fact is certain. Regardless of recent performance and future prospects, the financial institutions have their price. Should a bidder offer the opportunity for a quick, substantial profit, then professional investors are unlikely to support incumbent management. This view is also held by the Chairman of United Biscuits, Sir Hector Laing, whose company features heavily in the next case study. During the Nestlé–Suchard contest for Rowntree, he penned a leading article in *The Times* entitled, 'At any price it is still prostitution'. Laing concluded that 'in the present climate any and all of British industry is for sale if the price is right'. He called on fund managers to accept the 'the responsibility of ownership ... so that they are better serving the long term interests of the ultimate owners and the nation' (*The Times*, 2 June 1988). Perhaps the next major test of fund managers' 'responsibility' will arise from a foreign hostile bid for Allied-Lyons.

ISSUES AND LESSONS

When Elders' bid for Allied-Lyons was referred to the MMC, the fundamental issue was that Elders planned to break-up Allied-Lyons in order to reduce its debt. Divestment would have been essential to lower Elders' gearing. Not surprisingly, the OFT was concerned that such a major company should be dismembered by a much smaller bidding company, simply because it could not afford to keep Allied-Lyons intact. Employees and their trade union representatives were also concerned about job security and pension rights.

In the course of the MMC's investigation, however, Elders received a massive capital injection. Divesting the food division of Allied-Lyons was thus no longer a financial necessity. Elders had acquired a 20 per cent stake in BHP, Australia's largest company, which was a target of the Bell Group. As a result of this deal, Elders' balance sheet received a A$1 bn injection from BHP during the investigation, which was accepted by the MMC as security against the risks of high gearing.

The *Financial Times* certainly voiced the majority view in its editorial, 'Unwelcome form of takeover' (22 October 1987), but while it disapproved of the financing behind the bid, which it compared to 'junk bonds', it rightly concluded that 'there seems no issue here for the Monopolies Commission'.

The MMC's verdict confirmed that the bid should never have been referred in the first instance. Referring the bid succeeded in giving Allied-Lyons time to act, but it did little to enhance the reputation for consistency of UK merger policy.

The Elders versus Allied-Lyons battle was seen as a test case for leveraged bids, and thus some other companies regarded the MMC's clearance as a signal that leveraged bids would not be referred to the Commission. However, shortly after the MMC delivered its verdict, the Gulf Resources leveraged bid for Imperial Continental Gas was referred to the MMC by the Minister, simply because of the debt involved. This was a major factor in the more recent referral of the Goodman Fielder Wattie leveraged bid for Ranks Hovis McDougall. It could be argued, however, that the MMC should not have to investigate bids simply because of the form of financing used, and that this is rather a matter for the banking authorities to control, not merger policy enforcers.

As regards the companies involved in this battle, all appear to have benefited. Allied-Lyons has retained its independence, Elders acquired a large UK brewer, and Hanson Trust received a good price for Courage, which had been part of Imperial. Allied-Lyons is now a much more valuable company and has been forced to move faster than otherwise planned. In September 1986, its Chairman, Sir Derrick Holden-Brown, was reported as saying that 'Size is no longer a protection. The only defence that a public company has – and should have – is performance and prospects' (*The Observer*, 21 September 1986). More recent takeover bids may perhaps have caused him to revise that assessment.

TIMETABLE OF EVENTS
Elders vs Allied-Lyons

1985

22 February: Windemere Securities Ltd, later an associate of Elders, begins buying Allied-Lyons shares.

23 August: Sir Derrick Holden-Brown, Chairman of Allied-Lyons, writes to Elders seeking clarification of its intentions.

5 September: Elders admits it owns 7 m Allied-Lyons shares, and promises to clarify its position within six weeks. Allied-Lyons share price rose 18p on the day, to close at 285p.

22 September: Allied-Lyons begins its advertising defence campaign.

15 October: Elders announces that it has agreed with the Takeover Panel to clarify its position by 21 October.

21 October: Elders launches a £1.8 bn bid for Allied-Lyons.

29 October: Allied-Lyons suggests that Elders' bankers were contemplating illegal action.

30 October: Takeover Panel forces Allied-Lyons to retract allegation.

18 November: Elders issues its offer document.

2 December: Allied-Lyons issues its defence document.

6 December: The Minister refers the bid to the MMC. Elders' offer lapses, and Allied-Lyons' shares close at 270p, down 7p on the day.

1986

12 March: Elders sells its entire 6 per cent stake in Allied for £125 m or 306p per share.

24 March: Elders lodges an application for judicial review of the proposal made by Sir Godfray Le Quesne, Chairman of the Monopolies and Mergers Commission.

26 March: Elders given leave by the High Court to challenge the legality of the Monopolies and Mergers Commission's proposal.

31 March: Allied-Lyons signs a contract with Hiram Walker Resources Ltd, to acquire for a sum of C$2.6 bn (£1.2 bn) the spirits and wines division.

April: Elders sides with BHP which is a takeover target of Robert Holmes à Court's Bell Group.

Hanson Trust pays £2.6 bn for Imperial Group, including the Courage brewery and pubs.

23 April:	Hiram Walker Resources Ltd acquired by Gulf-Canada Corporation whose parent company is controlled by Reichmann Brothers.
8 May:	Allied-Lyons reveals 1985–86 pre-tax profits up 23 per cent at £269.5 m.
July:	Elders and BHP enter 20 per cent cross-equity links which strengthen Elders' capital base.
3 September:	MMC allows bid to proceed.
5 September:	Allied-Lyons signs £600 m deal with Reichmann Brothers for 51 per cent of Hiram Walker.
12 September:	Elders secretly offers £1.4 bn for Courage. Contract drawn up.
17 September:	Elders pays £1.4 bn for Courage.

Source: Press reports, in particular *The Observer*, 21 September 1986.

6

Hanson Trust Versus United Biscuits for Imperial Group

INTRODUCTION

On Monday 2 December 1985, the very same day that Argyll bid a record-breaking £1.9 bn for Distillers, Imperial announced its £1.3 bn agreed bid for United Biscuits. The following day GEC bid £1.2 bn for Plessey, and on the Friday, Imperial itself received an unsolicited £1.9 bn bid from Hanson Trust. In just five days, bids worth more than £6 bn had been announced. Britain had never seen so much bid activity before or since.

In February 1986, Imperial's bid for United Biscuits was referred to the Monopolies and Mergers Commission (MMC) on the grounds of competition in the snack food market. In order to overcome this hurdle, the two companies swapped roles and United Biscuits assured the Office of Fair Trading (OFT) that if successful it would reduce its market share by selling Imperial's Golden Wonder operation. This was the first time the OFT had ever allowed plea bargaining to avoid a referral.

The battle for Imperial was now between United Biscuits and Hanson Trust. The winner would be determined by the financial institutions. They would base their decision on the size of the offer, but also on the case presented by the management of the bidding companies.

In April 1986, Hanson Trust defeated the friendly bid from United Biscuits to acquire Imperial Group for £2.6 bn in the most expensive ever acquisition of a UK company. The financial institutions had rejected United Biscuits' and Imperial's vision of a British international food company able to compete with their much larger US rivals such as Philip Morris and RJR Nabisco, and European giants such as Switzerland's Nestlé and the Anglo-Dutch group Unilever, not to mention France's BSN, the largest Continental biscuit producer.

This case highlights the importance which the OFT attaches to domestic market share in reaching a decision on whether to recommend a referral to the MMC. At the same time, it charts the unprecedented flexibility of the OFT, and assesses its implications for companies and the regulatory authorities. Post-acquisition rationalization and its effect on employees are also briefly considered.

THE COMPANIES COMPARED

Imperial Group

Imperial was Britain's leading tobacco manufacturer, and held 40 per cent of the UK market. In addition to the tobacco division, it comprised two others: brewing and leisure, and foods. As Table 6.1 shows, in 1985

Table 6.1 *The companies compared, December 1985*

	Imperial*	United Biscuits†	Hanson Trust‡
Sales	£4.92 bn	£1.9 bn	£2.67 bn
Pre-tax profits	£235.7 m	£122.7 m	£252.8 m
Number of employees	70,000 approx.	41,467	64,000
Main interests			
Tobacco and confectionery: Players and Embassy cigarettes, Golden Virginia and St Bruno tobaccos, Famous Names liqueurs. Foods: Ross frozen foods Young's seafoods, HP and Daddies sauces. Brewing: Courage beers and pubs, John Smith's beers, Harp lager. Restaurants, hotels: Anchor Hotels, Harvester Steak Houses, Happy Eater restaurants.	Biscuits and confectionery: McVities, Ry-king, Crawford's, Macfarlanes, MacDonalds, Carr's biscuits, Terry's chocolates. Snack foods: KP nuts and snacks, own-label crisps. Frozen foods: McVities products. Restaurants: Pizzaland, and Wimpy chains. USA: Keebler cookies and crackers, Speciality Brand spices and herbs, Early California Olives.	UK retailing: Allders (formerly UDS) dept. stores, duty-free shops, shoe shops. UK manufacturing: Batteries (Ever Ready), bricks (London Brick, Butterley Building Materials), engineering (automotive equipment, meters, brewing equipment, industrial rubber, control equipment). US interests: fabric and yarn manufacturing, footwear manufacturing, food products, building products, furniture, lighting, miscellaneous industrial products.

Source: Financial Times, 9 December 1985.

*Year end 31 October 1985. †Year end 31 December 1985.
‡Year end 30 September 1985.

Imperial had annual sales of over £4 bn and its pre-tax profits were almost £236 m, an increase of 122 per cent since 1981. More than half of total sales and almost half of group profits stemmed from the tobacco division, but Imperial appreciated the need for product diversification into growth areas.

The tobacco industry was highly profitable, but it was not a growing business. Hence Imperial's rivals, the world's top cigarette manufacturers, were diversifying into other areas more in line with the health-conscious age. In 1985, America's and the world's two largest cigarette producers merged with food groups. Philip Morris, the industry's number one, acquired General Foods, and R. J. Reynolds acquired Nabisco, the world's largest biscuit manufacturer, and United Biscuits' great rival.

Imperial's early attempts to diversify had met with little success. None more so than the $630 m acquisition of America's Howard Johnson hotel and restaurant chain in 1980. This deal was a contributory factor to the boardroom coup in 1981, which saw Geoffrey Kent appointed Chairman. By 1985, Kent had been credited with having greatly improved the company's disappointing performance of the 1970s. But Imperial's recovery was held back by poor results from Howard Johnson, which was finally sold in the autumn of 1985 to the rapidly growing Marriott Corporation for $314 m, half the original purchase price.

Diversification remained a priority, and Imperial investigated 'a great number' of potential acquisition candidates before identifying United Biscuits as 'the selected partner' (Imperial offer document, 30 December 1985). Imperial was also well suited to the needs of United Biscuits, which required a steady cash flow. However, some commentators believed that the threat of an unfriendly bid was the main reason why Imperial was so eager to merge with United Biscuits. Lord Hanson wrote to Geoffrey Kent describing the deal as a 'reverse takeover' by United Biscuits. Later events suggested his interpretation of the United–Imperial deal was not inaccurate. In the same letter to Kent, Lord Hanson declared his interest in Imperial.

United Biscuits

Biscuit consumption per head in Britain is higher than in any other country. Perhaps this explains why United Biscuits was slow to expand abroad and enter new product areas, but in the early 1960s geographical and product diversification became priorities. United Biscuits needed a stronger international presence and a broader product range. However, penetrating a market which already has established brand leaders is very difficult. In the biscuit industry, as in others, acquiring a strong local firm is sometimes the only solution. Thus, in 1974 United Biscuits acquired Keebler, America's second largest biscuit manufacturer.

Similarly, America's Nabisco struggled in the UK market until it acquired Huntley and Palmer in 1982 for £84 m. With this deal, Nabisco became Britain's market leader in food snacks, and the number two biscuit manufacturer. This takeover had been referred to the MMC due to the possible effects on competition in the UK snack market. In its conclusion, the Commission said that 'any contemplated acquisition by the major suppliers which would increase the degree of concentration would merit careful scrutiny'.

United Biscuits' more recent US acquisitions had been of food (as opposed to biscuit) businesses, and by 1985 the US market accounted for more than 40 per cent of group sales, but Keebler was still responsible for the bulk (i.e. 92 per cent) of US sales. Sir Hector Laing, Chairman of United Biscuits, was increasingly aware of market potential in the Third World. But the world's second largest biscuit manufacturer needed cash to finance its plans to become a global player in the food industry. In Imperial it had found the ideal partner, but Hanson Trust stood in its way.

Hanson Trust

Hanson Trust is an acquisitive industrial conglomerate. It has grown rapidly since its stock-market flotation in 1964 to become one of Britain's largest companies, and within the next five years it may well become the largest. It has enjoyed 24 years of unbroken earnings per share, dividend and profit growth.

In 1985, Hanson Trust's turnover was little more than half that of Imperial, but Hanson's profit record was impressive. Hanson's profits were more than the profits of either Imperial or United Biscuits. Before acquiring Imperial, Hanson Trust's previous major acquisitions in Britain included Berec (i.e. Ever Ready) for £95 m (1982), UDS for £260 m (1983) and London Brick for £250 m (1984). In the USA, Hanson's two main acquisitions were US Industries for $571 m (1984) and SCM for $930 m in early 1986.

After an acquisition, Hanson usually recoups much of the original purchase price by well-chosen divestments, and retains those divisions capable of generating profits. For example, it sold SCM's Glidden Paints division to ICI for $580 m. Including other divestments, the SCM net price was little more than $100 m. Harvard Business School's Michael

Porter, the management guru of the 1980s, has singled out Hanson Trust as being successful in diversifying by acquisition (Porter, 1987). All of Hanson's main acquisitions have been of companies in mature, slow-growth sectors, with undervalued assets. Imperial was thus a typical Hanson target.

THE BATTLE

Imperial and United Biscuits had been convinced of the industrial logic of their agreed union. Each had what the other lacked. United Biscuits offered Imperial the opportunity to diversify away from tobacco, while the profits from Imperial's tobacco operations would allow United Biscuits to consolidate its position in the food industry.

A merged United–Imperial would have had almost 40 per cent of the UK snack market, a few points ahead of Nabisco, the market leader. A referral seemed likely, especially in light of the MMC's remarks at the time of the Nabisco/Huntley & Palmer takeover. But, on the other hand, sales of snack foods would have accounted for less than 5 per cent of total sales, and the basic rationale for the merger was to develop an international food company. Moreover, the OFT's own guide to mergers says: 'A merger which reduces competition in the UK may be justified in public interest terms from a strengthening of an industry's international competitiveness' (Office of Fair Trading, 1985b, p. 22).

Having weighed up these arguments, the Secretary of State, Paul Channon, referred Imperial's bid for United Biscuits to the MMC. By referring this bid, but not Hanson's for Imperial, the regulatory authorities had virtually conferred victory on Hanson Trust. The bid by Imperial automatically lapsed, and while the MMC conducted its investigation, which could take six months, Hanson Trust could acquire Imperial.

This seemed the likely outcome. However, United Biscuits, advised by Morgan Grenfell, was determined to merge with Imperial. It switched roles and bid for Imperial Group, a company twice its size. But merely swapping roles would not avoid a referral to the MMC. The United Biscuits bid would have to differ from Imperial's, and so it did. United Biscuits assured the OFT that if and when it acquired Imperial, it would reduce its share of the UK snack food market by selling its Golden Wonder operation. The OFT accepted this undertaking. For the first time in a British takeover, the OFT had accepted plea bargaining to avoid a referral.

United Biscuits had scored a notable victory, but at the same time a dreadful own goal. It agreed (conditional on a United Biscuits victory) to sell Golden Wonder to Dalgety for £54 m. As Hanson Trust pointed out, this was a 'knockdown price' – a view vindicated when Hanson sold Golden Wonder to Dalgety for £87 m.

On 17 February 1986, Hanson and United Biscuits launched their final offers for Imperial. Their value was determined entirely by the bidder's share value. Initially, United Biscuits had the edge on Hanson Trust, but during the next 21 days, the relative growth in Hanson's share price outpaced United's, narrowly giving Hanson the lead at the crucial moment. United Biscuits had set a closing date of 11 April, but it failed to win enough acceptances to take control of Imperial. Its offer was worth slightly less than Hanson's, and it seems fair to infer that the financial institutions had not been convinced that United and Imperial would become a successful international food group.

THE AFTERMATH

Since acquiring Imperial, Hanson has sold a number of Imperial's assets. Returns from recent divestments of Imperial's assets suggest that even at £2.6 bn, Imperial was a bargain. In September 1986, Courage was sold to Elders IXL for £1.4 bn. In this one deal alone Hanson recouped more than half of its outlay on Imperial. Golden Wonder was sold to Dalgety, not for £54 m as conditionally agreed with United Biscuits, but for £87 m. Hotels and restaurants were sold to Trusthouse Forte for £170 m and Finlay's newsagents were sold for £16.9 m.

United Biscuits has also benefited from Hanson's clear-out. It has boosted its frozen foods business with the purchase of Imperial's Ross and Young's frozen foods for £335 m in the spring of 1988. More recently, BSN, the French arch-rival of United in the biscuit war, expanded its other food interests with the £199 m purchase from Hanson of HP Foods and Lea and Perrins. Following this sale, it was estimated that the net cost of Imperial has been a mere £228 m (*The Sunday Times*, 17 July 1988), and Hanson still owns Imperial's highly profitable tobacco operations.

This has been satisfactory for Hanson and its shareholders, but not for some former Imperial employees. Under Imperial, the future of Golden Wonder's four manufacturing facilities had never been in question, according to officials of the Transport and General Workers' Union. However, shortly after Dalgety acquired Golden Wonder, two of the four plants were closed.

Trade unions have expressed concern that takeovers may adversely affect their members' pension schemes. These fears appeared to have been justified when it was discovered that with the sale of Courage to Elders, Hanson planned to transfer Courage pension scheme members to a new scheme to be established by Elders. They would take with them their legal entitlement plus £10 m of the surplus, with Hanson left holding £70 m, by far the bulk of the surplus. This plan was thwarted by the High Court which ruled that the committee of management of the three Courage pension schemes lacked the legal authority to sign deeds to approve the Hanson plan.

ISSUES AND LESSONS

During the takeover bid, Sir Gordon White, head of Hanson's US operations, ridiculed the idea of Imperial and United taking on America's food giants: 'We are just not big enough in this country' (*The Scotsman*, 25 March 1986). But the world's two largest food companies are not American. Unilever and Nestlé are both European, and they have each made a US acquisition worth $3 bn or more. Size, though, is not a prerequisite for success. For example, since failing to acquire Saint Gobain in 1968, France's BSN has been transformed from a glass company into France's leading food company and the world's leading producer of dairy products. Its growth in the food business continues with the acquisition, mentioned earlier, of HP Foods and Lea and Perrins, two of Britain's best-known brands.

Unlike their British counterparts, successive French governments have encouraged the creation of a French food giant. Thus, in 1986, BSN acquired Générale Biscuit, the largest biscuit producer in Continental Europe and third largest in the world. In the past three years, United Biscuits' two main rivals in the biscuit industry have either merged with, or been acquired by, a much larger group. United Biscuits thought it had found its partner, but it received little support from the enforcers of UK merger policy, and financial institutions certainly did not allow sympathy for the idea of United–Imperial as a national champion to influence their decision. However, even had United and Imperial merged, they would still have been dwarfed by the industry leaders (see Table 6.2).

Sir Hector Laing's disappointment that the financial institutions denied him the opportunity to achieve greater economies of scale is understandable. His challenge is to ensure that United Biscuits can be successful without necessarily being an industry giant, but he himself has so zealously preached the importance of size, that he may have convinced

Table 6.2 *The largest European and US food companies based on 1985 figures*

Company	Country	Annual sales ($ bn)
Unilever	Anglo-Dutch	21.62
Philip Morris–General Foods	USA	21.17
Nestlé	Switzerland	17.16
RJR–Nabisco	USA	13.53
United Biscuits and Imperial	UK	5.87*
Dalgety	UK	4.59
BSN†	France	3.16

Source: Fortune, 28 April 1986, 4 August 1986.

Fortune estimated Imperial's annual sales to be $3.40 bn. This probably underestimated Imperial's sales.
† Not including Générale Biscuit.

the market that United Biscuits itself is too small to succeed and that it, too, should be acquired.

In an age of global competition, when companies in many industries are convinced that 'big is better', the OFT appears in this case to have placed too much emphasis on UK market share, and disregarded the growing significance of the international dimension. The introduction of plea bargaining, however, is a welcome development, and its implications for companies and the regulatory authorities are considerable. This fact was not lost on Guinness which, like United Biscuits, was advised by Morgan Grenfell and took plea bargaining one stage further in its bid for Distillers.

The opportunity to divest the offending aspect of a takeover bid to avoid a referral to the MMC is likely to reduce the number of cases considered by the Commission. At the same time, this increases the already considerable workload and responsibility of the OFT.

TIMETABLE OF EVENTS

Hanson Trust vs United Biscuits for Imperial

Early 1984: Imperial begins screening process of acquisition/merger candidates.

1985

April: Imperial identifies United Biscuits as 'the preferred candidate' for a merger.

November: Imperial and United Biscuits agree to merge.

2 December: Imperial and United Biscuits announce agreed £1.3 bn merger

6 December: Hanson Trust launches record-breaking £1.9 bn hostile bid. Offer dismissed as 'ridiculously low' by Geoffrey Kent, Chairman of Imperial.

31 December: Imperial issues formal offer document for United Biscuits.

1986

3 January: Hanson Trust issues offer document

16 January: Imperial issues defence document.

7 February: OFT sends its recommendation to DTI.

10 February: Imperial attacks Hanson's US record.

12 February: Hanson bid allowed to proceed. Imperial's bid for United Biscuits referred to the MMC, in accordance with advice from the OFT.

13 February: United Biscuits has 14.9 per cent stake in Imperial. It paid £362 m for this stake, equal to its market capitalization at its lowest in 1981.

Imperial issues profit forecast of £290 m. Share price up 5p to close at 290p – 43p above Hanson's

16 February: Hanson's offer is worth 246p per Imperial share (i.e. £1.8 bn). Imperial's shares stand at 291p.

17 February: Hanson increases its bid from £1.8 bn to £2.32 bn. United Biscuits launches a £2.5 bn bid for Imperial. United Biscuits promises to sell Golden Wonder snacks and thus avoids a referral. Imperial's shares rise 29p to close at 328p.

Hanson forecasts a profit (pre-tax) of not less than £340 m for the year to end of September, an increase of 34 per cent on the previous year's performance.

19 February:	Hanson Trust says it will not increase its bid of £2.3 bn, which was already 28 per cent more than its original offer of £1.9 bn.
20 February:	Imperial's board recommends acceptance of United Biscuits' £2.4 bn bid.
27 February:	Hanson Trust tops United Biscuits' offer.
17 March:	Hanson Trust has 21 per cent of Imperial shares (first closing date).
24 March:	Hanson Trust has 26.9 per cent of Imperial (second closing date).
25 March:	United Biscuits says its offer of £2.55 bn is final and it will close on 11 April, rather than let the bid run its full course until 29 April as it is entitled to under the Takeover Panel's code. The United Biscuits offer is worth 337p. Hanson Trust's best offer is worth £2.7 bn or 361p.
	The Norwich Union believed to have already committed itself to Hanson Trust.
11 April:	United Biscuits fails to gain control of Imperial.
14 April:	Imperial directors recommend acceptance of Hanson's offer. Imperial's shares fall 18p to 345p, Hanson's by 8p to 177p and United Biscuits' by 2p to 265p. Hanson wins Imperial.

7

Guinness Versus Argyll for Distillers

INTRODUCTION

On 2 December 1985, Argyll, the grocery chain and drinks group, launched its then record £1.9 bn bid for Distillers, a Scottish company and the world's leading whisky producer, regarded by many as one of Britain's worst-managed businesses. However, on 20 January 1986 the Distillers board decided to recommend an offer from Guinness worth £2.2 bn. Only months earlier, Guinness had acquired Bell's, Britain's second largest whisky producer, and it came as no surprise, therefore, when Guinness's bid for Distillers was referred to the Monopolies and Mergers Commission (MMC).

An Argyll victory thus seemed certain, for an MMC investigation can last six months, even without an extension. Any celebrations in the Argyll camp proved premature, however, when Guinness persuaded the MMC that its bid had been dropped, and after consultations with the Office of Fair Trading (OFT) it launched a reformulated bid which avoided a referral to the MMC. Having overcome this hurdle, Guinness was back in contention in the battle for Distillers. The victor would be the highest bidder, but the value of each bid was in turn determined by the share price of Argyll and Guinness. On 18 April 1986, Guinness emerged triumphant, its offer worth £2.5 bn.

Months later, however, Guinness reneged on its promises regarding the appointment of Sir Thomas Risk as Chairman of the new group and the relocation of its head office to Edinburgh. This failure to honour its commitments was controversial enough, but it almost pales into insignificance compared to subsequent revelations. In early 1987, it was revealed that Guinness had used apparently illegal means to support its share price. The company was being investigated by inspectors from the Department of Trade and Industry, Ernest Saunders, its Chairman and Chief Executive, had been sacked and a number of fellow directors had been asked to submit their resignations.

This case study concentrates on four issues: Guinness's bid cost agreement with Distillers; the role of the OFT and the MMC; commitments given in takeover offer documents; and apparently illegal share support schemes. The revelations about Guinness's conduct in the battle for Distillers constitute 'the most far-reaching scandal ever known in the City of London' (Kochan and Pym, 1987).

THE COMPANIES COMPARED

Distillers

Distillers was Scotland's largest company, but although its headquarters were in Edinburgh, only four of the sixteen board members resided in Scotland, the others preferring to live in the South of England. In the course of the bid, the directors were labelled the 'Wentworth Scots'.

In recent years, white spirits had become increasingly popular, while worldwide consumption of whisky had fallen. Moreover, Distillers had seen its share of this declining market fall. At home, its share of the UK market had slumped from 75 per cent in the early 1960s to 15 per cent in 1984. By 1984, Britain's three best-selling whisky brands were owned by rivals of Distillers. Its performance in the global market was almost as unimpressive. Its market share slipped from 46 per cent in 1977 to 35 per cent in 1984, when only three of its brands featured in the twenty top-selling spirit brands – and these were less popular than in 1980 (see Table 7.1). Nevertheless, foreign sales still accounted for 90 per cent of group turnover and 95 per cent of profits.

Distillers was one of Britain's sleeping giants. *The Daily Telegraph* described Distillers as 'one of the worst-run large companies in Britain. In its way it is a classic British failure' (26 October 1985). By the summer of 1985, speculation was rife that Distillers was about to receive a hostile takeover bid. This coincided with similar reports concerning Allied-Lyons. The chairmen of both companies met to discuss the possibility of a merger, but talks were abandoned (Kochan and Pym, 1987). In 1985, Distillers reported profits of £236.2 m on sales of £1.274 bn. These profits are superficially impressive, but the City believed Distillers could have doubled them.

Argyll

Whether as a university student, a management consultant or a chief executive, James Gulliver, Chairman of Argyll, has always produced

Table 7.1 *1984's Top twenty spirit brands and owners worldwide (millions of cases)*

Brand		Owner	Category	Cases sold (million) 1980	1984	Average annual growth rate (%)
1	Bacardi	Bacardi	Rum	16.0	18.6	+ 3.8
2	Smirnoff	R. J. Reynolds	Vodka	13.6	13.5	− 0.2
3	Ricard	Pernod-Ricard	Anise	7.5	7.0	− 1.7
4	Suntory Gold	Suntory	Whisky	12.1	6.9	− 13.1
5	Gordon's Gin	Distillers	Gin	8.8	6.8	− 6.2
6	Johnnie Walker Red	Distillers	Whisky	7.0	6.4	− 2.2
7	Seagram's 7 Crown	Seagram	Whisky	7.0	5.6	− 5.4
8	J & B	Grand Metropolitan	Whisky	4.9	5.0	+ 0.5
9	Suntory Red	Suntory	Whisky	5.0	4.9	− 0.5
10	Jim Beam	American Brands	Whisky	4.4	4.8	+ 2.2
11	Bell's	Arthur Bell*	Whisky	4.8	4.3	− 2.7
12	Canadian Mist	Brown-Foreman	Whisky	3.1	4.3	+ 8.5
13	Presidente Brandy	Pedro Domecq	Brandy	3.9	4.2	+ 1.9
14	Ballantyne's	Hiram Walker	Whisky	3.4	4.1	+ 4.8
15	Canadian Club	Hiram Walker	Whisky	4.9	4.0	− 4.9
16	Jack Daniel's Black	Brown-Foreman	Whisky	3.4	3.9	+ 3.5
17	Popov	R. J. Reynolds	Vodka	3.8	3.8	−
18	Seagram's VO	Seagram	Whisky	4.6	3.7	− 5.3
19	Seagram's Gin	Seagram	Gin	3.6	3.7	+ 0.7
20	Dewars	Distillers	Whisky	3.9	3.5	− 2.6
	Total			125.7	119.0	− 1.4

Source: Financial Times, 13 January 1987.

*Purchased by Guinness, 23 August 1985.

outstanding results. In 1953, he graduated with a First in engineering from Glasgow University (where he is now a Visiting Professor in Management Studies), and twenty years later he won *The Guardian*'s Young Businessman of the Year award, in recognition of his success in transforming the Fine Fare supermarket chain. In 1965, when he took over, it was losing £300,000 a year. Seven years later it was making profits of £5 m.

Gulliver then left Fine Fare to establish his own company, and borrowed £1 m to buy a 30 per cent stake and a directorship in Oriel Foods. In 1974, America's RCA paid £11 m to acquire Oriel. Gulliver stayed at Oriel until 1977 when his firm, James Gulliver Associates, acquired Alpine, a double-glazing firm (RCA insisted that Gulliver agree not to enter the food business for three years). This venture provided Gulliver with yet another major success. In 1981, he entered the drinks business with the acquisition of Amalgamated Distilled Products, and repurchased Oriel Foods from RCA for less than £20 m. The following year, Allied Stores (Presto and other stores) – a company twice Oriel's size – was acquired for £104 m. In November 1983, Gulliver and his associates formed the Argyll Group.

By December 1985, Argyll's market capitalization was £670 m. Distillers was worth three times as much. For the year-end March 1985, Argyll returned profits of £53 m on a turnover of £1.676 bn.

Guinness

In 1961, Guinness's market capitalization was £87 m. Twenty years later it was just £3 m higher. The share price had slumped to 49p, reflecting years of stagnant profits (Pugh, 1987). Guinness needed a change in top management. Ernest Saunders was recruited from Nestlé of Switzerland.

Saunders's plan was to shed the motley assembly of unrelated, mainly loss-making businesses which had been acquired; rationalize the core businesses; and, finally, consolidate the leaner but fitter company's position in its key markets of drinks and, to a lesser extent, retailing (Kochan and Pym, 1987). A total of 149 businesses were divested at considerable cost. In 1982 alone, £49 m was written off in extraordinary items. The drinks industry was becoming increasingly concentrated. The best-selling brands were owned by a small number of companies. Saunders's plan was to create one of the largest international drinks companies. By the mid-1980s, this could only be achieved by acquisition. Other British companies (e.g. Allied-Lyons and Grand Metropolitan) were also intent on consolidating their position in the drinks industry. Saunders and Guinness therefore had to move quickly before opportunities for expansion were exhausted by rivals.

In June 1985, Guinness took its first step in the creation of a global drinks giant. It acquired Bell's for £356 m. Bell's had succeeded where Distillers had failed. In 1984, it had a 25 per cent share of the UK whisky market – compared to Distillers' 15 per cent – and the Perth-based company had just acquired the nearby, internationally renowned Gleneagles hotel and golf course.

The acquisition of Bell's was a solid starting point but in order to become an industry giant, Guinness had to acquire a firm the size of Distillers. The opportunity to acquire Distillers itself arose much sooner than even Saunders could have anticipated. By early 1986, Guinness had won many admirers in the City, and Saunders had cleverly deployed his marketing skills in cultivating influential journalists. The week before

Table 7.2   *The companies compared*

	Guinness*	Argyll†	Distillers†
Sales	£1.188 bn	£1.676 bn	£1.274 bn
Pre-tax profits	£86.1 m	£53.1 m	£236.2 m
Number of employees	13,647	36,800	14,900
Main interests	International beverages:	Food:	Scotch whisky:
	Guinness	Presto stores	White Horse
	Kaliber	Hinton's	VAT 69
	Bell's Whisky	Liptons	Haig
	Gleneagles Hotel	Templeton Galbraith	Johnnie Walker
	Retailing:	Cordon Bleu	White spirits:
	Lewis Meeson		Gordon's Gin
	R. S. McColl	Drink:	Booth's Gin
	Martin the Newsagent	Burberry's Whisky	Tanqueray Gin
	7–Eleven Stores	Barton brands	Cossack Vodka
	Richter Brothers	OVD Rum	
		Liquorsave	Food:
	Health care:		Yeast
	Portman Health Group		Frozen foods
	Nature's Best		Other:
			Carbon dioxide
	Publishing:		Glass
	Guinness Books		

Source: Annual reports.

*As at September 1985.
†As at March 1985.

bidding for Distillers, Guinness announced a 22 per cent rise in annual pre-tax profits to £86 m on a turnover of £1.19 bn for the year-end September 1985.

Table 7.2 compares Guinness with both Argyll and Distillers.

THE BATTLE

Bid and counter-bid: white knight to the rescue

On 2 September 1985, James Gulliver, Argyll's Chairman, issued a statement saying that Argyll did 'not intend to make an offer for Distillers at the present time'. The previous day, the Takeover Panel and Argyll had agreed that the company should not be permitted to bid for Distillers until 2 December.

This gave Distillers at least three months to erect its defences. Boardroom changes were made with the addition of some heavyweights, notably Sir Nigel Broackes of Trafalgar House. On 2 December, Argyll launched its then record bid of £1.9 bn for Distillers, which immediately rejected the bid as 'wholly unwelcome and inadequate'. Almost immediately, Guinness hatched its plans for a rival bid, but it was anxious that the bid would fail if it was referred to the MMC. Guinness met with Dennis Ford, then head of the Mergers Secretariat at the OFT. Ford had been involved in vetting Guinness's bid for Bell's and was well aware of the level of concentration in the UK whisky industry. He met with Guinness executives at the Guinness-owned Piccadilly Hotel in London, where he led the company's executives to believe that a Guinness bid would not be referred to the MMC.

On 9 January 1986, the Secretary of State for Trade and Industry, Leon Brittan, cleared Argyll's bid, in compliance with the recommendation of the Director General of the OFT, Sir Gordon Borrie. Distillers' management realized that it had little, if any, chance of remaining an independent company. The fight was no longer for independence but to find a 'white knight', and thus prevent an Argyll takeover. At the same time, with the acquisition of Distillers, Ernest Saunders of Guinness would achieve his strategic objective of transforming his company into one of the world's leading drinks companies.

On 20 January, Guinness launched its bid of £2.2 bn. Saunders said: 'I cannot seriously believe that anyone would stop this merger' (*The Money Programme*, BBC TV, 11 October 1987). In Guinness, Distillers had found its 'white knight', but Distillers' management had failed to realize its own strong bargaining position, and Guinness was allowed to dictate completely the terms of the merger. In addition, Distillers agreed to pay Guinness's costs. The capitulation of Distillers' management had been complete.

This cost arrangement threatened to double Argyll's costs, for if Argyll was successful in its bid, it would have to pay Guinness's costs as well as its own and those of Distillers. Argyll claimed this arrangement contravened Section 151 of the Companies Act 1985, while Guinness claimed it was permissible under Section 153 of the same Act. The Takeover Panel did not uphold Argyll's complaint.

On 6 February, Argyll increased its bid to £2.3 bn, and by doing so overcame Distillers' charge that its offer was inadequate, since the

Edinburgh giant had already accepted Guinness's offer of £2.2 bn. Argyll had every reason to be confident of victory. Guinness–Distillers would control almost 40 per cent of the British market for Scotch whisky. Most commentators were confident that the Guinness bid would be referred to the MMC, and that while it was in limbo, Argyll would be able to acquire Distillers.

MMC referral: plea-bargaining tactics

Paul Channon, the newly appointed Secretary of State for Trade and Industry, was married to a member of the Guinness family, and was a former director of the brewing company. In order to avoid any conflict of interest, his duties in this case were delegated to Geoffrey Pattie, the Industry Minister. On 14 February, Pattie complied with the OFT's recommendation and decided to refer the Guinness bid to the MMC. Ironically, it was Dennis Ford from the OFT who telephoned Guinness and informed them of the Government's decision.

Guinness's executives were stunned. A crisis meeting was held in the early hours of the morning at the company's Portman Square headquarters. Guinness telephoned Ford at his Southend home and said that they had sent a car to bring him to their headquarters. Two days earlier, the OFT had referred Imperial's bid for United Biscuits, but this hurdle was overcome by the two companies swapping roles and also by United Biscuits reformulating its bid to include an assurance to reduce its UK snack food market share. This satisfied the OFT, and the reformulated bid was not referred to the MMC.

Guinness took this tactic a stage further. It met with the MMC on four occasions in the three days 17–19 February, and persuaded Sir Godfray Le Quesne, the 62–year-old chairman of the Commission, that a referral of Guinness's bid but not Argyll's denied Distillers' shareholders the chance to choose between Argyll and Guinness (Kochan and Pym, 1987). Sir Godfray allowed Guinness to abandon its original offer and Guinness was once again a contender for Distillers. It raised its bid to £2.35 bn, and promised the OFT that five Distillers brands would be sold off in order to reduce UK market share to 25 per cent.

Argyll challenged the MMC's decision to lay aside the referral of Guinness's original bid in the High Court in London. It alleged that the mere divestment of a few brands was not sufficient to constitute a new bid under the 1973 Fair Trading Act, and that since Guinness had clearly not abandoned its bid, the referral to the MMC should still stand. But according to Mr Justice Macpherson, the new bid was 'so different in all important matters that it left the old bid behind like a discarded skin'. Therefore, laying aside the merger inquiry was not illegal and Sir Godfray had not contravened Section 75(5) of the Fair Trading Act 1973.

Argyll realized that a referral to the MMC would dash Guinness's hopes of acquiring Distillers. Argyll went to the Court of Appeal, but it did not find in Argyll's favour, despite the fact that it accepted that Sir Godfray was not legally empowered to decide himself to lay aside a reference. It also refused Argyll leave to appeal to the House of Lords.

The final duel

On 21 March, the revised Guinness bid was given the Government's all-clear. The battle for Distillers was now a straightforward fight between Argyll and Guinness. James Gulliver, Argyll's Chairman, was Scottish, and Guinness appreciated that it would have to match Gulliver's appeal to Scotland and its financial community in taking over a Scottish company.

In its formal offer document, Guinness accordingly promised to locate the new group's headquarters in Edinburgh with Sir Thomas Risk, Governor of the Bank of Scotland, as its chairman. However, while there can be no disputing Guinness's commitment to Sir Thomas, the statement regarding company headquarters was decidedly vague. The Guinness offer document said that 'We shall take the necessary steps to make the holding company a Scottish registered company and will move the group headquarters to Edinburgh where the group's chief executive office will be located.' Alf Young, one of Scotland's most respected business journalists, then writing for *The Scotsman*, retorted that Guinness's 'careful formulation is, frankly, not good enough. It may represent a genuine attempt to inject a new corporate vitality into Scotland. It may, equally, be a recipe for tokenism' (*The Scotsman*, 24 March 1986). Young's scepticism later proved to be well founded.

In the last few weeks of the takeover battle, Guinness's share price soared from just over 280p to over 350p at the critical moment, while Argyll's fell. By the end of April, after the battle was over, Guinness's share price had fallen to below 300p.

On 18 April, the final day of the bid, Guinness emerged as the winner, when just before 1 pm it announced that it held 50.78 per cent of Distillers' shares. Argyll had lost but, as James Gulliver said, 'Argyll's judgement last Autumn that Distillers needed a change of direction and new management have been fully vindicated.'

THE AFTERMATH

The drinks industry may have gone global, and Guinness's war cabinet was truly multicultural (for example, Saunders was Austrian, Furer Swiss, Roux French, Ward American). But Distillers was a Scottish company and some of the Scottish financial institutions had supported Ernest Saunders only after receiving an assurance that Sir Thomas Risk would be appointed non-executive Chairman of Guinness. Sir Thomas, in turn, had only agreed to accept the position on condition that group headquarters would be transferred to Scotland.

On 14 July 1986, Guinness shocked the financial community by announcing that 'it has not been possible to reach agreement with Sir Thomas Risk and he will not now be invited to join the Board nor therefore be nominated as non-executive Chairman'. Instead Saunders would occupy both positions of Chairman and Chief Executive. A bewildered Sir Thomas countered that he 'did not know the reasons for this decision nor on what issue Guinness have been unable to reach agreement with me'. Guinness claimed it disagreed with Sir Thomas on his role in running the company. Sir Thomas's desire to be actively involved in managing the group was at odds, Guinness said, with its intended passive role for him. Subsequent revelations about Guinness's apparently illegal conduct during the bid suggest that Guinness perhaps had more sinister reasons for breaking its promise of Sir Thomas's appointment. The Governor of the Bank of England, Robin Leigh-Pemberton, later commenting on this episode, said of Saunders, 'We now realise he has something to hide.'

Guinness appeared to have made a complete mockery of promises made during the takeover bid. Its behaviour suggested that companies could promise anything and everything to secure victory and then freely renege on these assurances. The Bank of England and the Stock Exchange failed to accept their responsibility to discipline Guinness, and simply passed the buck to Guinness's own shareholders. On 11 September, shareholders voted by a majority of 10–1 to accept the revised board structure which saw Ernest Saunders become Chairman and Chief Executive. However, a compromise was reached and a five-man committee of non-executive directors, with the same powers as a non-executive chairman, was created. It included two Scots, Sir Norman Macfarlane, Chairman of the Macfarlane Group and a director of the Clydesdale Bank, and Ian Chapman, then Chairman of William Collins, the publishers.

Arrival of the inspectors

On 1 December, David Donaldson QC and his team of Department of Trade inspectors arrived at Guinness's Portman Square headquarters – in London – to investigate the company's affairs. Over the next few weeks a catalogue of allegedly illegal and shady dealings involving Guinness was exposed.

On 12 December, Guinness's main US distributor, Schenley, revealed that at the end of the Distillers' bid its stake in Guinness had been more than 5 per cent. Failure to disclose its stake when the 5 per cent threshold was reached amounted to a breach of the Companies Act. Six days later, Guinness admitted that in May it had invested \$100 m (£69 m) in a speculative Boesky fund without notifying shareholders. But the real crisis erupted just after Christmas.

On 14 January 1987, the Guinness board announced that Ernest Saunders was being sacked, and that his closest advisers had either already resigned or been asked to submit their resignations. The next day, Sir Norman Macfarlane, the new Chairman, issued a letter to shareholders in which he explained that Guinness had acted illegally during the bid for Distillers. He disclosed that £25 m had been paid to unnamed advisers for 'advice and services believed to have been in connection with the Guinness bid'.

In 1981, when Ernest Saunders was asked to become Chief Executive of Guinness, the second choice had been Anthony Tennant of Grand Metropolitan, who had built Grand Met's International Distillers and Vintners subsidiary into one of the largest in the world. Six years later when Guinness was looking for Saunders's successor, the new Guinness board was in little doubt that Tennant was the man they wanted. In March 1987 he took up his appointment. Anthony Tennant said that the company's future strategy was to concentrate its resources on developing its international drinks business. Thus, in September 1987 Guinness sold its Martin's newsagents chain for £202 m to Panfida Ltd.

On 23 April 1987, Guinness made a £125 m write-off to cover the costs of 'unusual transactions and arrangements'. In September, it paid \$480 m to acquire Schenley, its US distributor, which had been at the centre of the scandal.

On 25 August and 2 September 1987, at hearings of the full Takeover Panel following the executive's investigations announced in January, the Panel determined that Guinness had been acting in concert with Pipetec, owned by Bank Leu in Switzerland, to purchase a block of Distillers shares at a higher price than Guinness was offering at the time of the bid to Distillers' shareholders in general. Under the *City Code*, Guinness would be liable to pay the higher price to all shareholders, at an estimated cost of £100 m. The Panel's decision has since been challenged in the courts with Guinness finally petitioning the House of Lords for leave to appeal over its application for a judicial review of the Takeover Panel's decision. This was rejected by the House of Lords Appeals Committee in November 1988. Guinness is now planning to appeal through the Takeover Panel's own appeal procedures.

On 2 October 1987, Sir Norman Macfarlane announced that Guinness would not be transferring its headquarters from London to Edinburgh. As one would expect, this was not a popular decision in Scotland, but fortunately for Guinness, the announcement coincided with news of two other transfers. The Guinness story was completely overshadowed by news of two of the biggest transfer stories in Scottish football: Richard Gough, captain of Tottenham Hotspur, signed for Glasgow Rangers in a £1.5 m deal, while rivals Celtic paid West Ham £800,000 for Frank McAvennie, the prolific goal scorer.

On 13 October, Ernest Saunders, who already faced charges of intent to pervert the course of justice and of destroying and falsifying documents, was charged with thirty-seven new offences relating to the Guinness takeover of Distillers. Ten were allegations of theft, ten of false accounting, ten of procuring the execution of a valuable security, two of common law conspiracies to manipulate the market in securities and five of enabling Guinness to provide financial assistance for the purchase of shares.

As of November 1988, the Guinness affair has led to a total of 105 charges against seven men. These are Ernest Saunders (42), Gerald Ronson, Chairman of Heron International (8), Sir Jack Lyons, the millionaire financier (9), Roger Seelig, former Morgan Grenfell corporate finance director and champion deal maker (19), Lord Spens, former head of corporate finance at the Henry Ansbacher merchant bank (4), Anthony Parnes, a former City stockbroker (19), and David Mayhew, a partner in Cazenove & Co, the stockbrokers (4). The trial of these men is now expected to take place in the summer of 1989.

ISSUES AND LESSONS

The Guinness scandal has highlighted some inadequacies of self-regulation in the City. The Takeover Panel has rightly tightened up its rules on disclosure and has also ruled to prevent other target firms from meeting the bidder's costs. But this dark episode in British business history leads to question marks over the Takeover Panel's current status. Opponents of a statutory body claim that the Panel's flexibility would be restricted, and that legislation would not be any more effective. However, the failings of self-regulation indicate that the Panel might benefit from having legal backing. While legislation *per se* will not eradicate excesses – the insider dealing scandal in the USA testifies to that – the Government has already shown itself ready to enact legislation simply because of the principle at stake (e.g. the ban on selling *Spycatcher* in Britain).

Regardless of the Takeover Panel's status, there is a specific need to ensure that promises contained in takeover documents should be legally binding. Shareholders base their investment decisions on information provided in these documents. Companies cannot be allowed to woo shareholders by promises which are then broken at will once victory has been secured. To permit such behaviour can only undermine the standing of the stock market and London as a reputable international financial centre.

Despite Guinness's subsequent conduct, the institutional investors – with one notable exception, Scottish Amicable – continued to support Ernest Saunders and Guinness. Wood MacKenzie, Guinness's stockbroker, and Charles Fraser, Chairman of Morgan Grenfell, Scotland, resigned their positions in protest at Guinness's failure to honour its commitments. Guinness's other advisers were unwilling to denounce publicly their client's conduct.

Guinness had allegedly breached the Companies Act, and such conduct already carries penalties of fines and imprisonment. Legislation already exists to punish those who were involved in Guinness's illegitimate activities. It is imperative for reasons of investor protection in general that perpetrators of any crimes committed either by Guinness employees, their advisers or supporters are brought to justice and that their punishment is sufficiently harsh to deter a repetition of such events.

Cash offers are rare in mega-mergers so the outcome of takeovers is determined by the share price of the bidder(s) and the target company. Thus, an increasingly large number of mega-bids have been decided by 'market muscle' – the ability of merchant banks to influence share prices. They may seek to inflate the share price of their client and deflate the share price of the opposition. This practice may lead bankers to engage in activities of dubious legality. A clearer definition is, therefore, required of share-buying operations which fall within the meaning of 'acting in concert'.

In the USA, some states have introduced laws which deny shareholders voting rights until they have owned shares for a stipulated period. The motive in these states is to curb hostile takeovers and encourage investors to adopt a longer-term perspective. Similar legislation, if for different reasons, may be desirable in the UK.

As regards merger policy, in contrast to the regulation of conduct during takeover bids, the main issue in this case was the MMC's decision to allow Guinness to abandon its original bid. This is unlikely to arise again, now that the principle of plea bargaining with the OFT has been firmly established, thus enhancing the flexibility of the referral decision process.

Guinness paid almost £3 bn for Bell's and Distillers. The acquisition of Scotland's two main whisky companies posed a threat to competition and the Guinness bid for Distillers was referred. Guinness reduced its projected market share by the disposal of five brands by Distillers for just £10.5 m. This was clearly a knockdown price. Sir Gordon Borrie said, 'I couldn't care less what the price was'. His sole concern was safeguarding competition, not the interests of Distillers' shareholders. Distillers' shareholders were already committed to paying Guinness's costs in the event of an Argyll victory, and now they were seeing five brands with 10 per cent of the UK market being sold for a mere £10.5 m to Whyte and MacKay, the Lonrho subsidiary. The introduction of plea bargaining to avoid a referral is welcome, but panic selling to avoid a referral, and especially, as in this case, when the outcome of the takeover bid was by no means certain, can hardly be in the interests of shareholders in the company whose assets are being sold off. Should further cases witness divestments at a bargain price, then perhaps the OFT should cease to encourage plea bargaining. It is also arguable whether by the divestment of five brands, Guinness was not merely temporarily reducing its UK market share. It is not inconceivable that the newly formed enterprise may decide to launch substitute brands, such as 'Son of Haig' for example.

The Guinness affair is a sorry episode with many hard lessons for the Government, the City and takeover combatants.

TIMETABLE OF EVENTS
Guinness vs Argyll for Distillers

1981

October: Ernest Saunders recruited to Guinness from Nestlé.

1982

January: Saunders becomes managing director of Guinness.

1983

November: James Gulliver and associates form Argyll Group.

1984

February: Gulliver considers takeover bid for Distillers.

1985

14 June: Guinness bids £330 m for Bell's.

23 August: Guinness wins control of Bell's.

1 September: Argyll agrees with the Takeover Panel that there will be no takeover bid 'at the present time' for Distillers. A three-month embargo is agreed.

2 September: Gulliver announces his intentions.

2 December: Argyll bids £1.9 bn for Distillers.

17 December: Argyll issues formal offer document.

30 December: Distillers issues defence document.

1986

9 January: Government announces that Argyll bid will not be referred to the MMC.

13 January: Distillers and Guinness discuss merger.

17 January: Sir Thomas Risk asked to be chairman of merged firm.

20 January: Guinness launches £2.2 bn bid. Distillers recommends acceptance.

27 January: Argyll complains to Takeover Panel over Distillers' agreement to pay Guinness's bid costs. Panel rejects complaint.

6 February: Argyll files writ alleging costs agreement is in breach of the Companies Act. It also raises offer to £2.3 bn.

14 February:	Guinness bid referred to the MMC.
19 February:	MMC agrees that the original Guinness bid can be dropped.
20 February:	Guinness mounts new bid worth £2.35 bn, and promises to divest five whisky brands.
25 February:	Argyll applies to courts for judicial review of the MMC's decision.
3 March:	Guinness issues formal offer document which includes commitment to appoint Sir Thomas Risk as chairman, and to locate head office in Edinburgh.
5 March:	High Court rejects Argyll's case. Stock Exchange introduces new rules to prevent a company from paying another's bid costs above 25 per cent of profits.
9 March:	Gulliver admits that he is not a graduate of Harvard, as his entry in *Who's Who* had indicated.
14 March:	Guinness sues Argyll and others over takeover advertisements.
15 March:	The Court of Appeal upholds High Court's decision. Argyll fails to have MMC's decision overturned.
21 March	OFT clears second Guinness bid. Five brands sold to Lonrho. Argyll raises bid to £2.5 bn.
18 April:	Guinness wins control of Distillers.
14 July:	Guinness says that Saunders will be chairman and that the board structure proposed in March has been dropped.
11 September:	At Guinness EGM, shareholders vote by a 10–1 majority to accept changes in board structure.
1 December:	DTI inspectors begin Guinness inquiry.
12 December:	Schenley admits failing to disclose it had a stake of more than 5 per cent in Guinness in latter stages of Distillers bid.
30 December:	Morgan Grenfell resigns as merchant banker to Guinness. Roger Seelig resigns from Morgan Grenfell.
1987	
9 January:	Saunders agrees to stand down temporarily during DTI investigation.
11 January:	Sir Norman Macfarlane appointed acting chairman.
14 January:	Guinness board announces sacking of Saunders as chairman of Guinness. Furer resigns as a director. US lawyer, Thomas Ward, asked to resign.

16 January:	Sir Norman issues letter to shareholders, confirming that Guinness had not complied with the Companies Act, and announces the existence of mystery £25 m invoice list.
20 January:	Christopher Reeves and Graham Walsh resign from Morgan Grenfell, in wake of pressure from Chancellor Nigel Lawson and Bank of England.
30 January:	Takeover Panel statement concerning breaches of City Code by Guinness.
18 February:	Anthony Tennant appointed chief executive of Guinness.
6 May:	Saunders arrested in London.
12 May:	Saunders appears in court and is remanded on bail of £500,000.
26 May:	Saunders submits resignation as a director of Guinness.
September:	Guinness acquires Schenley for $480 m.
2 September:	Takeover Panel determines that Guinness had acted in concert with Pipetec, owned by Bank Leu of Switzerland, to purchase a block of Distillers shares at a higher price than Guinness was offering to Distillers' shareholders in general.
2 October:	Guinness confirms that it will not be moving corporate headquarters from London to Edinburgh.
Note:	Since October 1987, a number of prominent businessmen have been arrested in connection with the Guinness takeover of Distillers. Ernest Saunders faces further charges. As of November 1988, these men continue to await trial, now expected to take place in the summer of 1989.

8

GEC Versus Plessey

INTRODUCTION

On 3 December 1985, the day after Argyll and Imperial launched their billion pound-plus bids for Distillers and United Biscuits respectively, GEC, Britain's largest manufacturing company, proposed a £1.2 bn merger with Plessey, its smaller but main rival in the UK electronics and telecommunications market. The following month, Leon Brittan, in one of his last major decisions before resigning as Secretary of State for Trade and Industry over the Westland affair, referred GEC's bid to the Monopolies and Mergers Commission (MMC). Seven months later, by a majority of 5–1, the MMC ruled that the bid was not in the public interest. This view was accepted by Paul Channon, Leon Brittan's successor, and GEC's bid was blocked.

This case raises once again the issue of striking the correct balance between competition in the domestic market and the international competitiveness of UK firms. The disproportionate decline in Britain's share of world trade and manufacturing is rightly a cause for concern. What is particularly disturbing is that current government policy has been criticized as a contributory factor. Moreover, the source of this criticism has been one of the Conservative Government's strongest allies – the Confederation of British Industry (CBI).

According to Sir Gordon Borrie, Director General of the Office of Fair Trading (OFT), 'the CBI believe that mergers policy can conflict with the objective of promoting international competitiveness' (Borrie, 1987a). The CBI argues that in order to compete internationally, UK firms must have a 'critical mass', which may require a single company so large that competition within the UK market is impossible. It contends that the primary objective of government policy should be 'the improvement of the UK's international competitiveness' (Borrie, 1987a). Sir Gordon, on the other hand, disagrees that competition policy should be sacrificed. He argues the exact opposite, namely that the stimulus of competition in the domestic market is a prerequisite for international success.

THE COMPANIES COMPARED

Plessey

The 1960s was a critical decade in Plessey's history. Through a series of acquisitions, Plessey diversified into solid-state technology, as well as civil and military communication systems, military radar and traffic control. In 1982, it consolidated its position in telecommunications with the acquisition of America's Stromber-Carlson Corporation (Monopolies and Mergers Commission, 1986).

The size discrepancy between GEC and Plessey is highlighted by the fact that Plessey's turnover of £1.4 bn in 1985–86 was only twice the size of GEC's profits. Plessey's turnover and profits were one-quarter the size of GEC's, and Plessey's labour force of 34,000 was just less than one-fifth of that of GEC.

GEC

In the seven cases covered in this book, the bidding company has often been smaller, in terms of sales, than the target (e.g. Elders for Allied-Lyons, United Biscuits for Imperial, Argyll and Guinness for Distillers, Dixons for Woolworth). In this case, GEC, the bidding company, was much larger than Plessey, the target (see Table 8.1). Indeed, GEC is Britain's largest manufacturer, with more than 160,000 employees. Its interests are also much more diverse than those of Plessey (see Table 8.1). In 1986, group turnover was almost £6 bn, and pre-tax profits amounted to over £700 m.

GEC's current size owes much to Lord Weinstock who became Managing Director in 1963 when GEC's profits were just £6.1 m. In 1967, GEC acquired Associated Electrical Industries (AEI) and the following year it merged with the English Electric Company Limited, overcoming a rival bid from Plessey. The product overlap between GEC and the acquired companies, plus industry overcapacity, demanded a massive rationalization and restructuring programme in the late 1960s and early 1970s with the loss of over 70,000 jobs.

In 1979, another two major acquisitions were completed: A. B. Dick Company of Chicago, and Averys, Britain's leading manufacturer of weighing and measuring equipment. Other acquisitions were made during the 1980s, including Yarrow Shipbuilders in 1985.

Table 8.1   *The companies compared, 1986*

	GEC	Plessey
Sales	£5.97 bn	£1.46 bn
Pre-tax profits	£700.6 m	£170.2 m
Number of employees	164,536	34,366
Interests	Electronic systems and components Telecommunications and business systems Automation and control Medical equipment Power generation Electrical equipment Consumer products Distribution and trading	Telecommunications and office systems Electronic systems and equipment Engineering and components

Sources: Company annual reports; MMC (1986) Report on the proposed merger.

GEC and Plessey overlapped in telecommunications, but liberalization of the telecommunications market had led to intense competition as new suppliers emerged, including foreign multinationals. Recent years have seen the formation of strategic alliances and mergers in the industry, most notably the merger of ITT's European telecommunications interests with those of France's CGE, in the belief that collaboration and pooling of resources were essential for those wishing to remain internationally competitive.

The UK's share of world telecommunications exports has declined from 25 per cent in the early 1960s to 5 per cent in 1986 (Monopolies and Mergers Commission, 1986). In the UK, GEC and Plessey together accounted for about one-third of British Telecom's (BT) purchase contracts placed in 1984–85, and 50 per cent of this expenditure was on purchases of the System X digital switching equipment. BT, like GEC and Plessey, believed there were 'significant advantages' to be gained from merging the two companies' telecommunications businesses.

Both companies accepted the need to integrate their telecommunications business, but neither side could agree on how this would be achieved. This failure to agree resulted in GEC bidding for Plessey. The offer was rejected, but Plessey offered to buy GEC's interests in System X.

While GEC and Plessey hold a strong position in the UK telecommunications and defence market, internationally they are both small fry (see Table 8.2). GEC is ranked 10th in the world telecommunications league table, and Plessey 12th. By merging, the newly formed firm would only

Table 8.2 *Major companies (ranked by total group sales) in the defence electronics, telecommunications and electronic systems markets*

Rank	Company	Country	Group sales in 1984–85 ($£$ m)	Company	Operating profits before interest and tax as a percentage of sales, 1984–85 (%)
1	IBM	USA	38,700	IBM	24.4
2	AT & T	USA	27,959	GTE	19.0
3	General Electric Co	USA	23,544	Fujitsu	12.4
4	Siemens AG	FRG	14,046	Northern Telecom	10.8
5	Philips	Netherlands	12,935	Daimler-Benz	10.5
6	GTE	USA	12,255	General Electric Co	10.2
7	Daimler-Benz	FRG	11,793	**GEC**	**10.1**
8	ITT	USA	9,409	**Plessey**	**10.1**
9	Westinghouse	USA	8,647	Motorola	9.0
10	NEC	Japan	7,673	AT & T	8.5
11	RCA	USA	7,305	Gould	8.4
12	CGE	France	6,569	Honeywell	7.5
13	Fujitsu	Japan	5,308	L. M. Ericsson	7.4
14	**GEC**	**UK**	**5,222**	Philips	7.1
15	Thomson	France	5,128	NEC	6.8
16	Honeywell	USA	5,117	AEG AG	6.6
17	Motorola	USA	4,662	Westinghouse	5.9
18	AEG AG	FRG	2,986	ITT	5.5
19	L. M. Ericsson	Sweden	2,794	RCA	5.2
20	Northern Telecom	Canada	2,793	CGE	4.9
21	Plessey	**UK**	**1,416**	Siemens AG	2.9
22	Gould	USA	1,179	Thomson SA	1.9

Source: Monopolies and Mergers Commission, 1986.

move to 9th in the league, one-fifth of the size of America's AT & T (see Table 8.3). Thus, a merger of the two firms would have had a negligible effect in international terms. There is little doubt that the telecommunications business of both Plessey and GEC was small, and that their rivals were becoming bigger as the industry underwent significant rationalization.

However, most of the major developments have been in international alliances and cross-border takeovers. Indeed, the strategic advantage in this type of tie-up seems more enlightened than merely buying up one's domestic competitor. It must be stressed that whether growth is pursued organically or by domestic or foreign acquisition or collaboration, size *per se* is no guarantee of success. For example, Sweden's L. M. Ericsson is only half the size of GEC, yet it has enjoyed outstanding success in telecommunications.

In 1985–86, GEC was the Ministry of Defence's (MOD) largest

Table 8.3   *Leading world manufacturers of telecommunications equipment*

Company	Telecommunications sales, 1984 (£ m)
AT & T (USA)	7,590
ITT (USA)	3,500
Siemens (West Germany)	2,530
Northern Telecom (Canada)	2,460
L. M. Ericsson (Sweden)	2,380
NEC (Japan)	2,010
Alcatel-Thomson (France)	1,935
GTE (USA)	1,710
Philips (Netherlands)	893
GEC (UK)	**746**
Fujitsu (Japan)	744
Plessey (UK)	**677**
Italtel (Italy)	470

Source: Monopolies and Mergers Commission, 1986.

supplier, and Plessey was the fourth largest. Together the two companies received 15 per cent of total MOD payments. The MOD was concerned that 'there was a risk that a merger would produce a company that would try to exploit the domestic defence market, buying up further competitors in a bid for total market domination'.

THE BATTLE

On 3 December 1985, GEC proposed a merger with Plessey, but the offer was rejected. Three days later GEC informed Plessey that a bid would proceed 'as soon as possible', and on 9 December it announced its bid. The formal offer document was issued two days before Christmas.

On 31 December 1985, Plessey started legal proceedings against GEC in the USA. Early on in the takeover battle, Plessey sought to enlist the help of the American courts to frustrate GEC's hostile bid. Plessey argued that the GEC takeover offer applied to its US shareholders in Plessey and sought an injunction requiring GEC to conform to US securities laws. GEC denied that its offer had been made to Plessey's 3,000 US shareholders, who held 1.6 per cent of Plessey's shares.

In an unequivocal judgement, the Delaware District Court refused an injunction. The judge stated: 'It is at least possible that Plessey's efforts in this litigation are motivated more by a desire to delay than to inform. This court, therefore, concludes that it would be a perversion of the principles of the Williams Act [governing takeover bids] to delay the process of a quintessentially British takeover when American interests and investors are but barely touched' (*Financial Times*, 18 January 1986).

According to GEC, the Plessey defence document of 13 January 1986 contained false and misleading statements which were seriously defamatory. GEC thus started libel proceedings against Plessey and three directors – Plessey Chairman, Sir John Clarke, Peter Marshall and Warren Sinsheimer. GEC's wrath had been incurred mainly by what it alleged was a calculated misquotation of the Chairman of the House of Commons Committee of Public Accounts in connection with the Tigerfish torpedo and also a quotation from stockbrokers De Zoete Bevan 'which is so highly selective as to amount to a blatant misrepresentation'. Proceedings were initiated only after Plessey refused to issue a correction and an apology.

On 20 January 1986, the Secretary of State, Leon Brittan, referred GEC's bid to the MMC. In early August, it was announced that the MMC had ruled by a 5–1 majority that the bid was against the public interest, and the bid was blocked.

ISSUES AND LESSONS

Apart from those divisions of the Department of Trade and Industry concerned with the industrial sponsorship of the electronics and telecommunications industries, the proposed merger had met with widespread opposition from both companies' suppliers and competitors, plus customers, unions, local authorities and MPs. But the Ministry of Defence was the main critic of the merger. It argued that its costs would increase as a result of the reduction in competition.

The MMC's report on the proposed merger reflected the Government's policy that mergers should be referred to the MMC 'primarily' on competition grounds. The report concentrates almost entirely on the competition implications of the proposed merger. This emphasis was welcomed in an editorial in the *Financial Times:* 'the commission reached the right decision for the right reasons' (*Financial Times*, 7 August 1986).

The Department of Trade and Industry favoured a merger between GEC and Plessey because it would have produced a bigger group able to compete in world markets. Five of the six-strong investigators of the MMC sided with the Ministry of Defence whose argument against the merger centred on increased costs because of reduced competition. The majority report of the MMC thus blocked the GEC–Plessey merger.

The sole dissenting voice of the MMC was C. C. Baillieu who argued that the majority report failed to give 'sufficient weight' to three important considerations:

(a) the size, sophistication and essentially monopolist powers of the two major United Kingdom customers, BT and the MOD;

(b) the international dimension of the markets for both telecommunications and defence electronics where overseas competition in price and quality can no longer be ignored; and

(c) the size of the development effort needed for the next generation of equipment which will be beyond the capability of any one national grouping, let alone any one company.

(Monopolies and Mergers Commission, 1986)

The lesson to be learned from this case, according to the Director General of the Office of Fair Trading, is that 'when the Commission is assessing claims that a merger will lead to improved efficiency it will be looking for substantive evidence, not mere assertion'. At the same time, the issues raised by C. C. Baillieu would seem worthy of more serious consideration.

By way of sequel to this case, Plessey is once again under attack from GEC. But this time it is in the form of a bid of £1.7 bn in combination with Siemens of West Germany. The EC context of the bid is a major justification put forward by GEC's Chairman, Lord Weinstock, who said 'we are going to have a single European market and there is an industrial dimension to that' (*Financial Times*, 17 November 1988). Whether or not Plessey will survive this time remains to be seen.

TIMETABLE OF EVENTS

GEC vs Plessey

1985

3 December: GEC proposes £1.2 bn merger with Plessey, which rejects the offer.

9 December: GEC bids for Plessey.

23 December: GEC issues formal offer document.

31 December: Plessey starts legal proceedings against GEC in the USA.

1986

13 January: Plessey issues formal defence document. GEC starts libel proceedings against Plessey.

20 January: GEC's bid referred to the MMC.

6 August: MMC blocks GEC's bid. Plessey retains independence.

Source: Press reports.

9

Dixons Versus Woolworth

INTRODUCTION

In October 1982, Paternoster Stores acquired the UK stores of Woolworth for £310 m from the US parent company. Following the acquisition, Paternoster Stores changed its name to Woolworth Holdings (hereafter referred to as Woolworth).

Less than four years later, in April 1986, Dixons launched its £1.75 bn bid for Woolworth. In this case, the large financial institutions owned virtually all Woolworth's shares. The five largest shareholders held more than 40 per cent of the share capital. The future of Woolworth thus lay in the hands of the institutions, and their verdict would be determined by recent performance and future prospects. Dixons launched its bid just days before the Takeover Panel's clamp down on 'knocking copy', but advertising is aimed mainly at the small shareholder, so its absence had no bearing on this takeover.

The crucial issue throughout this takeover battle was whether institutional investors would continue to support the Woolworth's management team, headed by Sir John Beckett, which they had backed since the 1982 acquisition of Woolworth's UK operations. Since then, Woolworth management had already provided tangible evidence of its success, but nagging doubts remained as to whether they had done enough to retain the backing of the institutions. In reaching their decision, the financial institutions had to assess the respective retailing strategies of each firm.

THE COMPANIES COMPARED

In recent years, the retail trade has been among the most dynamic sectors of the UK economy. Many of Britain's best-known stores have changed hands as acquisitive retailers seek to transform dowdy, boring stores into shops which are both attractive and exciting. Already some of the larger

Table 9.1 *The companies compared, 1985–86*

	Dixons	Woolworth
Sales	£943.4 m	£1.7 bn
Pre-tax profits	£78.1 m	£81 m
Number of employees	11,651	52,000

Sources: Annual reports; *The Sunday Times,* 1 June 1986.

takeovers have fallen short of expectations. In 1987, just two years after merging, Asda–MFI decided to part company. Similarly, Sir Terence Conran's Storehouse group – the result of a £1.5 bn merger between BHS and Habitat-Mothercare – received two hostile bids in three days at the end of September 1987, following disappointing results. The larger of the two was a £2 bn all-share bid from Benlox Holdings, an engineering and investment dealing group worth only £45 m!

In bidding for Woolworth, Dixons was proposing to acquire a company nearly twice its size in terms of turnover (see Table 9.1).

Woolworth

Apart from the high-street stores of the same name, the Woolworth group at the time of the takeover bid included Comet, the electrical goods discount chain, and B&Q, the DIY and gardening group. During its first three years, Woolworth's new management had an impressive track record. The value of the original investors' stake had increased tenfold, and profits had risen sharply. But Woolworth management had never underestimated its task. From the outset in 1982, it had said it would take seven years to achieve a turnaround.

In 1986, the main challenge facing the group was restructuring Woolworth's stores. In earlier decades the success of Woolworth's high-street shops had been mainly due to its reputation for low prices – after all, the shops were known as 'the sixpenny store' (nothing in the store cost more than sixpence). By the 1980s even the most mundane items had become status symbols and consumers often spurned cheaper products for more expensive ones.

In March 1986, the dual-pronged 'Operation Focus' was launched. It was designed to solve Woolworth's fundamental problem: sales of £127 per square foot were too low. The new strategy was designed to double that figure. First, the number of product lines would be rationalized, and the group would concentrate on only six ranges: basic DIY and gardening items; children's wear and toys; confectionery; records, cassettes and video tapes; table and kitchenware; and toiletries. Profits would hopefully rise by achieving higher sales volume. The food and adult clothing lines were to be abandoned. Second, management recognized that Woolworth owned two different types of store, very large units and small high-street shops. In order to draw customers' attention to the difference, the 200 major stores would be called 'Weekend Woolworth' while the remaining 600 smaller ones would be known as 'Woolworth General Stores'.

Dixons

Stanley Kalms, Chairman of Dixons, is very much a self-made man. His business career began at the age of 16, in 1948, in his father's photographic studio. Foreseeing the decline in portrait photography he began selling cameras instead, but he was also one of the first UK retailers to introduce cheaper models from the Far East. Dixons went public in 1962 and is now one of Britain's best-known chain stores. In addition to Currys, it has acquired Power City, Mastercare and, most recently, Supasnaps.

In late 1984, Dixons had acquired Currys, its main electrical rival, after a bitterly fought £232 m contest, which ended with Currys conceding defeat in the High Court. The Dixons chain, which sells a host of electrical gadgetry – but notably not 'white goods' – has established a niche as the market leader for hi-tech buffs. Had it gained control of Woolworth, Dixons would have ranked as Britain's sixth largest retailer.

THE BATTLE

Dixons had been eyeing up Woolworth ever since the new management had taken over, almost four years earlier. The final decision to mount a bid was taken on Good Friday – 28 March – after Woolworth's 1985 annual results had been announced. Although profits were up 43 per cent to £81 m, Dixon's Chairman, Stanley Kalms, believed the results confirmed that Woolworth 'had clearly run out of ideas'. Senior management and Warburg, Dixons' merchant bank, were summoned immediately to prepare the offer which was made less than one week later.

On Thursday 3 April 1986, Dixons launched its £1.75 bn bid for Woolworth. Woolworth's Chairman of just one month, Kenneth Durham, found that his first few months at the helm would prove even more demanding than he could have anticipated. During the bid

Woolworth's main spokesman was Chief Executive, Geoffrey Mulcahy, who had been promoted in 1984 from the position of Finance Director.

The offer was rejected by Woolworth and Dixons knew that it faced a battle likely to prove as ferocious as when it had captured Currys. Nonetheless, victory seemed likely. Throughout the bid, Kalms was highly critical of Woolworth's management ('There is not a retailer among them' – a remark that prompted Woolworth to issue a writ against Kalms claiming injurious falsehood) and of the stores ('There is no design in the Woolworth shops to make them attractive. People go in for their "pick & mix" sweets, spend a quid and then they are off'). So why was Kalms so eager to gain control of Woolworth?

If Woolworth's stores themselves were drab, their prime site locations were very appealing. Kalms would sell three product ranges in Woolworth stores: goods for the home, the garden and entertainment products. He would cease to sell clothes and food. Kalms and his advisers had also learned from the experience of United Biscuits and Guinness with the Office of Fair Trading (OFT). Despite its obvious attractions, Dixons promised to sell Comet in order to escape a referral to the Monopolies and Mergers Commission (MMC). The buyer was later identified as Granada.

In June, the Secretary of State for Trade and Industry announced that Dixons' bid would not be referred to the MMC. The promise to divest Comet had satisfied the OFT that, if successful, Dixons would not have an excessive market share in retailing electrical goods. By the final week of the battle, Dixons was no longer as confident of clinching victory. It relaxed the condition that it should obtain 90 per cent of Woolworth's equity, and now declared that the bid would be unconditional if it won 50 per cent (Dunn, 1987).

On 2 July the bid closed and Dixons had secured just 35.6 per cent of Woolworth's shares. It had failed to gain control of the much larger retail group.

ISSUES AND LESSONS

This case was a turning point in the spate of mega-mergers. All the previous mega-mergers which had not been blocked by the MMC had seen the target company lose its independence. Woolworth had successfully warded off a hostile bid without recourse to a 'white knight'. By backing Woolworth, the financial institutions, which held 90 per cent of Woolworth shares, had refuted allegations of 'short-termism'. Apparently only one of the ten largest Woolworth shareholders supported Dixons.

Dixons' promise to divest Comet showed how quickly firms had learned to package their bids in order to avoid a referral to the MMC. By promising to divest certain assets, bidders can be virtually assured that their bid will be allowed to proceed. The critical hurdle in merger policy is now increasingly the OFT. In terms of merger policy, the MMC has become almost obsolete.

TIMETABLE OF EVENTS
Dixons vs Woolworth

1986

12 March:	Both sides deny rumours of bid.
3 April:	Dixons launches £1.75 bn hostile bid for Woolworth.
28 April:	Dixons issues offer document.
8 May:	Woolworth issues defence document.
22 May:	Dixons announces that it has agreed to sell Comet to Granada, conditional on its bid being accepted.
1 June:	Dixons announces Operation Ramrod.
10 June:	Minister announces that bid will not be referred to the MMC.
18 June:	Dixons issues revised offer document.
19 June:	Woolworth issues final defence document.
30 June:	Dixons announces that the conditions of its offer have been changed. It will now be conditional on acceptances of over 50 per cent instead of 90 per cent.
2 July:	Dixons controls only 35.6 per cent of Woolworth's shares. Bid fails.

Source: Dunn (1987).

10

BTR Versus Pilkington

INTRODUCTION

BTR's bid for Pilkington in late 1986–early 1987 'crystallised a national debate on the industrial impact of the merger wave' (*Financial Times*, 21 January 1987).

Pilkington was seen as the paternalistic employer, committed to research and development, whose long-term planning and pursuit of technical excellence had seen the north-west based firm become the world's leading glass manufacturer. In its formal defence document, Pilkington argued that the bid was about 'the future of *all* British companies who believe in the creation of wealth and the pursuit of excellence that leads ultimately to world leadership – rather than the poverty of cashing in the future for short-term financial gains'.

The Pilkington view was accepted by numerous Members of Parliament (MPs) who denounced BTR as an acquisitive conglomerate whose short-term horizons and lack of research and development (R&D) posed a threat to Pilkington and its employees. The impact of a BTR takeover on the regional economy of the North-West also became a major issue. Some MPs argued that the takeover should be referred to the Monopolies and Mergers Commission (MMC) simply because it entailed a transfer of control from the North-West to the more prosperous South-East.

This case will show that this portrayal of BTR was an unfair distortion. The company had certainly grown and diversified by acquisition, but its past record indicated that it was not an asset stripper. BTR was a company doctor, rather than a corporate axe-man, whose rigidly enforced prescription had nursed ailing patients (e.g. Dunlop acquired in 1984 for £101 m) to a full recovery. Even when it had divested a business, it considered carefully the likely consequences for employees involved. For example, in 1983 it acquired Thomas Tilling, itself a conglomerate which owned Cornhill Insurance. Three years later, BTR decided to sell Cornhill – and only then because it did not think insurance fitted in with its other businesses – but it consciously sold to Allianz, the West German company, in order to guarantee job security for Cornhill employees. Of course, this was not an entirely altruistic gesture. BTR did not wish to be seen as an asset stripper, because it believed that such a reputation could be exploited by one of its future target companies. Why then was BTR so maligned during the battle for Pilkington?

It is very likely that BTR was the victim of changing attitudes to takeovers. Its bid for Pilkington was a year too late. Until the spring of 1986, the positive aspects of takeovers were readily accepted. The City was glad to see Distillers' management ousted and replaced by Ernest Saunders who had revitalized Guinness. It hoped he would achieve similar results with the whisky giant. However, the reputation of Saunders had been bruised by his failure to adhere to promises given in the heat of the battle, and worse was to come. Shortly after BTR announced its bid, the Guinness scandal broke. It could scarcely have picked a more inopportune moment to launch a takeover bid.

With the Guinness scandal raging, takeover activity and regulation in the City became major political issues. Politicians clamoured for less of the former and more of the latter. Thus, the BTR–Pilkington takeover battle became 'one of the most politically contentious' in recent years, as MPs lobbied for a referral to the MMC (*Financial Times*, 21 January 1987). Despite intense political pressure, Paul Channon, the Secretary of State, stuck to government policy and refused to refer the bid to the MMC. Thus, the market rather than the Government determined the outcome of the bid.

In its previous acquisitions, BTR had paid generous premiums to secure victory (e.g. 86 per cent for Huyk in 1980, 71.1 per cent for Serck in 1981 and 84.4 per cent for Thomas Tilling in 1983). When BTR announced its bid on 20 November 1986, its offer was worth 545p per share, and Pilkington's shares were worth 530p. This represented a premium of just under 3 per cent, but during the bid the value of Pilkington's shares soared. In this instance BTR was unwilling to match the market's valuation of Pilkington, let alone pay a premium. On 22 January 1987 BTR withdrew its bid. Pilkington had successfully retained its independence.

THE COMPANIES COMPARED

Pilkington

Pilkington had been guided through the 1980s by Antony Pilkington, who became Chairman in 1980. Under his leadership, the company had become the world's largest glass producer. This position had been attained partly through international takeovers in Europe – Flachglas of West Germany was purchased for £141 m from France's BSN in 1980 – and in the USA where it acquired Libbey-Owens-Ford (LOF), the US number two, in a $250 m (£170 m) deal in the spring of 1986. LOF's glass division had sales of $690 m in 1985, almost 50 per cent of which went to its main customer, General Motors (*Financial Times*, 11 March 1986).

Like other European companies, Pilkington had found acquisition the only way to achieve significant penetration of the US market. (In August 1987 its US base was further strengthened with the purchase of Revlon's optical division for $574 m (£361 m).) The LOF purchase saw Pilkington increase its world market share from 12 to 18 per cent, leapfrogging PPG of the USA with 17 per cent, and Saint Gobain of France with about 13 per cent, to occupy pole position.

In 1986 Pilkington, with a workforce of almost 45,000, returned profits of almost £106 m on sales of £1.32 bn (Table 10.1). In the late summer its share price began to rise as an associate of BTR built up a small stake. By early November rumour was rife that BTR was about to bid. The acquisitive conglomerate had not made a major acquisition in the UK for over two years. Its past record suggested a takeover bid was overdue.

BTR

Prior to its bid for Pilkington, BTR had invariably mounted a bid when

Table 10.1 *The companies compared, 1986*

	Pilkington*	BTR†
Sales	£1.32 bn	£4.02 bn
Profits	£105.8 m	£504.8 m
Number of employees	44,700	79,400
Interests	Glass and optical equipment	Energy and electrical equipment, construction, transport, industrial products, health care, paper, printing, sport, leisure

Source: Annual reports.

* Year end 31 March 1986.
† Year end 31 December 1986.

the target company was at its most vulnerable. For example, Thomas Tilling's profits peaked at £81.1 m in 1979, but in 1982 they had fallen to less than £44 m. The time was ripe to strike, and in a narrow victory in 1983, BTR acquired Tilling, which itself had been a very acquisitive industrial company. Before the bid, BTR had a market capitalization of £1.05 bn and Tilling's stood at £358 m. Ten days after the acquisition, the enlarged BTR was worth £1.87 bn. This represented an increase of £461 m on the sum of the market capitalization of the two firms before the bid.

BTR's success can be attributed to an acquisition programme which has developed dominant market positions in the company's core businesses and skills. Its core businesses were rubber, plastics and metal manufacturing, and industrial marketing was its forte. Strong market shares in new areas had been developed through sequential, related acquisitions.

Apart from the individual merits of the two companies, this takeover battle was often presented as a contest between two opposite corporate cultures. BTR has obviously been aggrieved by some of the characteristics attributed to it. For example, it used its 1986 annual report to correct any misconceptions. It stressed that its expenditure on research and development had been substantial, and that its employees were evenly distributed throughout the UK, and not just concentrated in the South of England. A complaint was also brought by Sir Owen Green against Coopers and Lybrand, Pilkington's auditor, about an attack on the company's accounts in the course of the takeover bid, which alleged that there were weaknesses in BTR's profit and cash flow record. However, this complaint was not upheld by the disciplinary committee of the Institute of Chartered Accountants in England and Wales.

THE BATTLE

On Thursday 20 November 1986, BTR ended weeks of speculation and launched a £1.16 bn takeover bid for Pilkington just six weeks before Sir Owen Green was due to vacate the Chief Executive's chair. Sir Owen told *The Observer*: 'Our offer is based on the assumption that Pilkington will report pre-tax profits of up to £220 m for the year to next March.' This statement proved critical later when Pilkington issued its profit forecast, which was much better than the City had expected.

According to one commentator, opposition to the BTR bid 'assumed the dimensions of a religious crusade' (*The Sunday Times*, 18 January 1987). On Merseyside, Pilkington enjoyed the overwhelming support of its employees, the community and local politicians. At the same time, Pilkington found strong support from the Labour Party and Conservative back-benches. In their efforts to gain a referral to the MMC, these sympathizers exerted pressure on the Secretary of State for Trade and Industry and/or the Director General (DG) of the Office of Fair Trading (OFT).

Those in favour of a referral admitted that the takeover would not have led to further concentration in the UK glass industry, as BTR has no existing interests in the sector. Their argument was based on employment considerations, the regional dimension and the view that BTR would not promote research and development. On 15 January 1987, the Government followed the advice of Sir Gordon Borrie, Director General of the OFT, and decided not to refer the bid to the MMC. Paul Channon's decision was very unpopular even among his own back-benchers. Indeed, three Junior Ministers at the Department of Trade and Industry – Giles Shaw, Geoffrey Pattie and Alan Clark – criticized Channon for not referring the bid to the MMC. One Conservative MP, Michael Grylls, Chairman of the Trade and Industry Committee of Tory MPs, said that the Pilkington decision had brought the Government's merger policy 'into disrepute'. The Opposition leader, Neil Kinnock, accused the Government of permitting 'a destructive merger mania to imperil British manufacturing industry' (16 January 1987).

A further source of embarrassment for the Government was the rise in Pilkington's share price in the afternoon prior to its announcement that the bid would not be referred. Only a few weeks earlier the DTI had launched an inquiry into leaks of share price-sensitive information by civil servants, and in particular those at the OFT.

BTR had overcome the referral hurdle, and the outcome would now be determined by shareholders. The following day, Pilkington announced a profits forecast of £250 m. This was much better than the most optimistic expectations of analysts. Pilkington's shares received another boost and stood at 710p, against BTR's offer of 547p. Clearly the offer had no chance of success.

Less than one week later BTR withdrew its bid, having decided not to increase its offer. Sir Owen Green explained that 'Our conclusion is that the revision necessary for a bid to succeed would now involve a price, for a cyclical business, greater than any which could lie within the best interests of BTR shareholders. We will therefore allow our bid to lapse.'

ISSUES AND LESSONS

Pilkington, like Allied-Lyons, has certainly benefited from receiving a hostile bid. Apart from its positive effect on the share price, it highlighted Pilkington's failure to communicate effectively its achievements to the City – its share price was as low as 315p at one point in 1986. The company has since adopted a high profile and, like a number of other British companies, has launched a TV commercial campaign to increase public awareness of the company and its products. The importance of effective communications and the disclosure of as much information as possible, within competitive limits, about corporate financial performance and prospects cannot be overstressed if a 'correct' or fair valuation is to be placed on a company's shares.

The repeated incidence of leaks, apparently from the OFT, is a matter of serious concern. It is suggested that OFT recommendations are perhaps best given verbally to the Secretary of State for Trade and Industry.

Some members of the present Government believe that BTR's decision to withdraw its bid for Pilkington was a vindication of the Government's view that issues other than competition are best left to the markets. Paul Channon, in a speech to the Centre for Policy Studies conference on industrial policy, said that it was 'surely right that in general it should be the shareholders and not bureaucrats who should decide ownership of companies'. The Government clearly believes that the function of merger policy is to safeguard competition. Thus, the only guiding principle for the OFT and the MMC must be competition. Whether or not the balance between domestic and international competition is correct remains open to question. But UK merger policy, like that in the USA, is perhaps better for concentrating simply on competition. The OFT and MMC should not be expected to forbid mergers because of some supposed lack of 'industrial logic', or because of alleged deficiencies in a particular management team.

As long as the UK persists with a merger policy which includes grounds other than competition, the Secretary of State, the OFT and the MMC will be subject to lobbying in every major takeover battle. The decision not to refer BTR's bid was important, because it showed that merger policy is based primarily on competition, not the extent of political lobbying. A policy based simply on competition will continue to attract criticism, but if it is consistently applied, lobbying *per se* will become an unrewarding activity. The extent of lobbying in recent takeovers is unlikely to be repeated if the Government consistently conforms to its

TIMETABLE OF EVENTS
BTR vs Pilkington

1986

3 September: Pilkington shares stand at 428p.

4 Sept.–10 Oct.: An associate of BTR begins buying Pilkington shares at prices of between 423p and just over 457p, and builds up stake of 3.4 per cent.

8 November: Pilkington's share price rises as speculation mounts that a BTR bid is in the pipeline.

20 November: BTR mounts £1.16 bn bid which Pilkington immediately rejects as having 'no industrial, commercial or financial merit'. BTR's offer worth 545p per share, amounts to a premium of just 3 per cent over Pilkington's share price of 530p.

Pilkington share price rises 81p on the day to close at 611p.

8 December: Pilkington announces 76 per cent increase in interim pre-tax profits to £87 m.

10 December: Pilkington issues formal defence document.

12 December: BTR formally attacks Pilkington's defence – 'an exercise in complacency'.

15 December: MPs attack BTR's bid for Pilkington.

17 December: Having received only 0.05 per cent acceptance, BTR extends its offer to 24 January – the 60th day of the bid – the date the offer must close under the timetable stipulated by the Takeover Panel's City Code. Pilkington share price rises 3p to 641p.

24 December: Pilkington strengthens its defence team with the appointment of a second public relations adviser, Broad Street Associates.

1987

2 January: Timetable for BTR bid extended by Takeover Panel due to delay in decision whether bid should be referred to the MMC.

7 January: Unions back Pilkington.

8 January: Further political pressure for a referral.

14 January: Pilkington's shares rise 20p in the late afternoon to close at 651p.

15 January:	Government decides not to refer the bid to the MMC. Pilkington's shares rise 33p to 684p.
	BTR demands an urgent Stock Exchange inquiry into a 'precipitate increase' in Pilkington's share price on the eve of the announcement.
16 January:	Pilkington issues another defence document including a £250 m profit forecast, much better than City expected. Share price rises 25p to close at 710p. Analysts believe BTR will have to increase its offer from 545p to 800p if it hopes to win.
22 January:	BTR abandons its bid.

Source: Chikoti (1987).

own policy statement, as it did in the BTR–Pilkington case.

Neither should merger policy act as a surrogate branch of regional policy. Companies from one region in the UK should be free to acquire those in another. If restrictions based on the location of company headquarters were imposed on takeovers involving UK companies, then consistency would demand that such measures apply to foreign acquirers. Britain's open-door foreign investment policy should be preserved provided other major countries do the same and provided UK merger policy develops in a way which encourages, or at least does not deter, the development of strong UK companies better able to compete internationally. To do otherwise could have serious adverse effects on the national economy.

11

Nestlé Versus Jacobs Suchard for Rowntree

INTRODUCTION

In recent years, the confectionery industry, in common with the food industry as a whole, has become increasingly concentrated. As will be seen below, the major confectionery companies have been busy acquiring others in a bid to strengthen their brand portfolios. Despite the industry's move towards globalization, the confectionery market has not yet become standardized. Considerable differences in consumer tastes have survived despite the efforts of confectionery manufacturers. For example, in Continental Europe, slabs or solid bars of chocolate have been preferred by consumers, unlike the UK market where 'count-line' products (i.e. individually wrapped chocolate-coated bars) are much more popular.

The European chocolate and confectionery market is worth an estimated £5.25 bn per year, almost one-third of the world total. Any company wishing to be a major player in the global chocolate and confectionery industry must, therefore, have a strong presence in the large European market. Within Continental Europe, West Germany and France are the two largest markets, and these, along with the markets of The Netherlands, Italy and Benelux countries, are dominated by three firms. These are Switzerland's Jacobs Suchard, Mars of the United States and the Italian company Ferro Rocher, which together have a combined market share of between 60 and 80 per cent in each of these markets.

The UK market is also dominated by three companies but two of these are domestic firms. The market leader is Cadbury Schweppes with 30 per cent of the chocolate and confectionery market, followed by Mars with 26 per cent and then Rowntree with 24 per cent. These three companies produce all but 7 of the 50 top selling chocolate and confectionery brands in the UK. Promoting these brands is expensive. Cadbury Schweppes accounted for 31 per cent of the £100 m spent on all chocolate and confectionery advertising in 1987. Mars, the biggest spender in 1986, was overtaken by Rowntree, and slipped to third place on 25 per cent. The Mars Bar and Rowntree's Kit-Kat remain the world's two most popular 'count-line' brands. In 1986 'count-lines' accounted for 51 per cent of all chocolate and confectionery sales in the UK, though this figure dropped to 46 per cent in 1987.

Given the UK market structure, acquisition was the only way for another company to emerge as a significant player in the British chocolate industry. Hence, Cadbury Schweppes has been under threat of takeover since 1986 when General Cinema of the USA became its largest shareholder. For the time being, Cadbury Schweppes is still independent, but Rowntree, its arch rival, was acquired by Nestlé in June 1988. The deal was eventually recommended by Rowntree management, but only after its efforts to resist Nestlé, and another Swiss company, Jacobs Suchard, had proved unsuccessful. In this case, the UK Government ignored arguments for referral, stressing that neither bid posed a threat to competition in the UK market.

THE COMPANIES COMPARED

Rowntree

Based in York, and renowned in Britain as a paternalistic employer, Rowntree's origins can be traced back to the late nineteenth century when Joseph Rowntree founded the company. During the depressed interwar years, the company struggled, only to be revitalized by a succession of new products which still remain among the company's best-selling brands. In the 1930s the following brands were all introduced: Black Magic (1933), Dairy Box and Aero (1934), Kit-Kat (1935) and Smarties (1937). After the Second World War, other successful brands were launched, and the company attracted a hostile bid from overseas during the merger boom of the 1960s.

In 1969, Rowntree was a takeover target of America's General Foods, itself recently acquired by Philip Morris for $5.6 bn. However, charitable trusts established by the founding family owned 50 per cent of the shares and Rowntree retained its independence. Later that year, Rowntree merged with another UK confectioner, Mackintosh, the effect of which was to reduce the trusts' stake in the merged firm to less than 7 per cent.

In the early 1960s, Rowntree had launched an export drive to Continental Europe. Manufacturing facilities were acquired in West Germany (1963) and France (1970), but progress was slow due to production and marketing difficulties, and European operations had to be reorganized in 1985. By the late 1980s, Rowntree believed it had overcome its problems, with products such as After Eight and Lion Bar proving highly successful in France and West Germany. By 1987, sales on the Continent amounted to £300 m, or just over 20 per cent of total turnover (see Table 11.1) returning profits of £11 m – a poor profit margin compared to the UK level.

Rowntree had also concentrated on developing its presence in the US market in a series of acquisitions, most notably the purchase of Sunmark, the St Louis-based confectionery manufacturer, for $230 m in August 1986. As a result of these deals, North American sales represented 28 per cent of total turnover of £1.29 bn in 1986, a sizeable increase from 6 per cent in 1980. Penetrating the US chocolate market was a formidable challenge. Not only did Mars and Hershey control 70 per cent of the market, but Hershey had licences to make and sell in the USA, Rowntree's two best-sellers, Kit-Kat and Rolo.

Like numerous other British companies, Rowntree had had its share of disappointments with US acquisitions. Prior to Sunmark, its largest US purchase had been Tom's Foods, the crisp and snack food maker, for £137 m in 1983. Diversification into snacks proved unsuccessful though, and in January 1988 Rowntree announced its plans to sell off Tom's Foods along with its UK snack food interests. The proceeds of the sale were intended to bolster the 'core' confectionery business, by providing funds for acquisitions, but before a buyer had been found Rowntree itself had received two hostile bids.

Although Rowntree at last appeared to be making progress on the Continent, many professional investors remained unimpressed by its profit record. For many years, Rowntree executives had stressed that they were pursuing a long-term strategy. By the spring of 1988, the City had clearly decided that Rowntree had met with limited success. It valued the company at less than £1 bn. This evaluation of Rowntree and its brands was much less than that of the two Swiss bidders. The opportunity to earn

Table 11.1 *Rowntree: breakdown of sales by markets (%)*

Country/region	1986	1987
UK and Ireland	41.5	39.7
Continental Europe	20.1	21.0
North America	27.9	29.1
Australasia	4.0	4.2
Rest of world	6.5	6.0

Source: Annual reports.

a hefty profit on selling Rowntree's shares was tempting to institutional investors, regardless of their appraisal of the incumbent management.

Jacobs Suchard

In 1982, in Switzerland's largest ever takeover, the Jacobs coffee business merged with Interfood, the parent company of the chocolate companies Suchard and Tobler. Since the merger, sales have risen from S.Fr 4.5 bn in 1983 to S.Fr 6.1 bn (£2.4 bn) in 1987, and net profit has risen from S.Fr 110.2 m to S.Fr 265.3 m. The company has grown to become Europe's second largest confectioner. The Zurich-based company is headed by Klaus Jacobs who has been responsible for shaping the company's long-term strategy. Indeed, corporate objectives are enshrined in Vision 2000, his idea of Jacobs Suchard at the end of this century. Of course, Jacobs has recognized that his company is much smaller than major rivals, such as Mars and Nestlé, both of which have strong global operations. In order to compete against these giants, Jacobs Suchard has had to diversify geographically, and to lower costs to compete effectively.

Long before its bid for Rowntree, Suchard had indicated its global aspirations. With more than 90 per cent of its 1986 sales based in Western Europe, it was important to increase sales in North America, home of the confectionery industry's numbers one and two, Mars and Hershey, respectively. Hence in early 1987, Suchard paid $730 m to acquire E. J. Brach, America's third largest confectioner, from American Home Products. At the same time, it widened its brand portfolio in Europe with the purchase of Côte d'Or, Belgium's celebrated producer of luxury chocolates, for S.Fr 190 m (£74 m). It also acquired the Italian producer Du Lac, which had manufactured the Milka, Suchard and Tobler brands under licence. Despite its major US acquisition, 83 per cent of total group sales still came from the European market (see Table 11.2).

In order to achieve its second objective, to become the industry's lowest-cost manufacturer and marketer, production had been rationalized and management decentralized. Capital spending exceeded net profits in each year during the period 1982–85, as production of individual brands was concentrated on fewer factories and plants were closed at San Sebastian, Stuttgart and Paris. The level of automation was greatly increased and the responsibility of brand managers considerably increased.

In 1987, 43 per cent of total sales were still derived from the coffee business, Jacobs. This dependence on a commodity whose price is subject to dramatic fluctuations provided Suchard with a strong reason to

Table 11.2   *Jacobs Suchard: breakdown of sales by markets (%)*

Country	1983	1984	1985	1986	1987
West Germany	43.7	39.3	39.9	44.9	37.9
France	21.4	24.2	25.3	25.0	20.7
Switzerland	12.7	13.9	13.3	6.3	5.0
Rest of Europe	15.6	15.5	14.7	16.6	19.1
Total Europe	93.4	92.9	93.2	92.8	82.7
North America	5.3	5.4	5.4	5.9	16.6
Other	1.3	1.7	1.4	1.3	0.7

Source: Annual reports.

expand its confectionery business. Moreover, although it had successful brands such as Milka, Suchard, Toblerone, Tobler and Côte d'Or, these had a negligible share of the UK market. The company's key markets were West Germany (37.9 per cent of total sales) and France (20.7 per cent) (see Table 11.2).

In both these crucial markets, Rowntree had also been busy pursuing market share by promoting heavily its brands which had proved so popular in the UK. The Yorkshire-based company, therefore, not only posed a major obstacle to Suchard penetrating the lucrative UK market, but it also threatened to win market share in France and West Germany, at the expense of Suchard.

Another major influence on Suchard's recent expansion through acquisition, and its bid for Rowntree, has been the Swiss management's recognition that confectionery, despite national differences in consumers' palates, is a global industry. The bid for Rowntree was quite unrelated to '1992'. As Charles Gebherd, senior group vice-president said: 'We cannot just focus on 1992 in Europe, we need global marketing and advertising' (*Financial Times*, 14 October 1987).

Nestlé

Based in Vevey, this Swiss multinational dwarfed both Rowntree and Suchard, and indeed was considerably larger than the two combined (see Table 11.3). In 1987, its turnover of over S.Fr 35 bn was almost six times greater than that of Suchard. Excluding sales of non-food items, Nestlé ranks as the world's largest food company, and is among the thirty largest corporations in the world.

Nestlé comprises some eleven divisions, but drinks and dairy products account for almost 50 per cent of total sales. Geographically, its activities

Table 11.3   *The companies compared, 1987*

	Rowntree	Jacobs Suchard	Nestlé
Sales	£1.43 bn	S.Fr 6.1 bn	S.Fr 35.24 bn
Pre-tax profits	£112.1 m	S.Fr 418.3 m	S.Fr 1.83 bn
Number of employees	33,120	16,053	163,030
Main interests	Confectionery, incl. Kit-Kat, Quality Street, Smarties, After Eight. Sun-Pat. Snack foods, Tom's Foods. Retail companies.	Confectionery, incl. Suchard, Tobler, Côte d'Or, Milk. Coffee.	Drinks. Dairy products. Frozen foods and ice cream. Chocolate and confectionery. Refrigerated products, Infant foods and dietetic products. Food service products. Hotels. Petfoods. Pharmaceutical products. L'Oreal activities.

Source: Annual reports.

are concentrated in Europe and North America. In 1987, these two markets accounted for more than 70 per cent of sales (see Table 11.4). In 1987, it had more than 163,000 employees. While its international activities represent a critical factor behind its success, during the 1970s the company's reputation was bruised by the infamous baby food scandal. Nestlé's marketing of its powdered baby milk in Third World countries was heavily criticized by various pressure groups, especially in the USA, which argued that it was an inappropriate substitute for breast milk in countries where purified drinking water was not readily available, and where illiterate consumers were prevented from following the instructions provided, concerning the correct use of the product. Rowntree, on the other hand, was renowned in Britain as an exemplary employer, whose Quaker origins were reflected in its paternalistic approach to current and former employees.

Happily for Nestlé, it has been spared the controversy which dogged it in the 1970s. In 1981, the German-born Helmut Maucher was appointed Managing Director. In his first five years in office, sales increased by 70 per cent and trading profits have increased even faster, by 110 per cent. Prior to the Rowntree bid, Maucher had made two major acquisitions. In

Table 11.4 *Nestlé: breakdown of sales by markets (%)*

Region	1986	1987
Europe	39.7	43.1
North America	31.2	28.5
Asia	13.4	13.0
Latin America & Caribbean	10.6	10.0
Africa	2.9	3.0
Oceania	2.2	2.4

Source: Annual reports.

1985, Nestlé paid $3.0 bn to acquire Carnation, in the largest ever Swiss takeover of a US company. In the spring of 1988, it sought to consolidate its European food operations with the purchase of Buitoni from Italy's Carlo de Benedetti, who was embroiled in a hostile bid to acquire Belgium's largest company, Société Générale de Belgique. The outcome of this takeover awaits approval by the French monopolies board, which is investigating the proposed deal because of its effect on Buitoni's French shareholders. Mounting another large acquisition so quickly after the move for Buitoni did not pose a problem to Nestlé with its large liquid reserves.

Suchard's efforts to build itself a stake of shares in Rowntree had placed the UK company into play. The chance to add Rowntree's brands to its own confectionery interests was too tempting an opportunity to miss. On 26 April 1988, Nestlé entered the game with a £2.1 bn bid.

THE BATTLE

On 13 April 1988, Warburg Securities mounted a 'dawn raid' for Rowntree, on behalf of Jacobs Suchard. By 9.15 am it had spent £162 m, 629p per share, acquiring a 14.9 per cent stake in Britain's second largest confectioner. Although Suchard had succeeded in becoming the single largest shareholder in Rowntree, it ruled out a full bid for at least a year, unless another party mounted such a bid. Almost two weeks later, Nestlé offered £2.1 bn for Rowntree. The bid was rejected immediately by Rowntree's Chairman, Kenneth Dixon.

Now that Rowntree, a long-established successful UK company, was faced with a hostile bid from overseas, an intensive political campaign to stop the takeover took off. The case was debated in the House of Commons, and in the letters pages of the business press. The major issue to emerge from these discussions was 'reciprocity'. The argument put forward by many was that the bid should be prohibited because while Swiss companies could acquire UK companies in hostile bids, the shareholding arrangements of some Swiss companies were such that they were safe from predators. Even the Director General of the Confederation of British Industry (CBI), John Banham, argued that Rowntree should remain British. He added his support to those who called for a level playing field in international takeovers. His intervention was, not surprisingly, ill-received by Nestlé, a member of the CBI for more than 30 years, which also had 19 plants in the UK and 10,000 employees. This debate tended to be clouded by the misunderstanding that Swiss legislation prohibits foreign takeovers of Swiss companies.

Switzerland, like most countries, has no merger controls, and legally any company, domestic or foreign, is free to acquire another. Indeed, in the course of the Rowntree bid, Switzerland's most prestigious watchmaker, Piaget, was acquired by France's Cartier. The legal attaché of the Swiss Embassy in London explained that 'In those cases where a takeover seems difficult or impossible, it is down to the internal articles of association of the company, which just express the will of shareholders not to be bought out.' Nevertheless there has been a sharp rise in merger activity in Switzerland during the 1980s (see Chapter 1). The Swiss delegate to the Organization for Economic Co-operation and Development (OECD) Committee on Competition Law and Policy, which met only days before Nestlé secured control of Rowntree, attributed the increase partly to the 'internationalization of markets'.

Despite the political clamouring for a referral, Sir Gordon Borrie, Director General of the OFT, decided that there was no justification for referring either the Nestlé bid or Suchard stake to the MMC. His advice was accepted by Lord Young, the Secretary of State for Trade and Industry, who had argued consistently that UK companies were free, like some Swiss enterprises, to constitute their share structures in such a way as to make themselves bid-proof. Indeed, some UK companies (e.g. Great Universal Stores, Savoy Hotel and Trusthouse Forte) have such defences in place. Lord Young's decision not to refer the Nestlé and Suchard cases to the MMC was a major disappointment for the Rowntree management. Its defence strategy had concentrated on winning a referral. Rowntree's days of independence were clearly limited, and Kenneth Dixon began holding secret talks with both Nestlé and Suchard in order to identify the better 'partner'.

On 26 May, the day after Lord Young gave both Swiss companies clearance to proceed with current or proposed bids, Suchard launched a £2.3 bn bid for Rowntree. In the following weeks, the 'reciprocity' debate continued. The Government was accused of placing a 'For sale' sign on 'Britain PLC'. Finally, on 23 June, Nestlé gained control of Rowntree when it made a £2.62 bn bid and the board of the UK company recommended that its shareholders should accept this offer.

THE AFTERMATH

The Nestlé/Rowntree takeover ranks as one of the largest ever deals in the UK, and is by far the largest UK takeover by a foreign company, overtaking Elders' £1.4 bn acquisition of Courage. Nestlé, at a stroke, became the world's largest chocolate company, overtaking Mars. Rowntree management, employees and shareholders also appear to have done well from the deal. Nestlé has established a chocolate division and Kenneth Dixon, the Rowntree Chairman, has been promoted to Nestlé's General Management Committee with responsibility for the new division. Rowntree is still based in York and headed by the same management team. In the course of the bid, Rowntree's shares more than doubled in value, benefiting the 6,000 employees with shares in the company.

Even the defeated Jacobs Suchard has not come away empty handed. It decided to sell its 29.2 per cent stake in Rowntree, and made a profit of more than £200 m. Despite this 'consolation prize', defeat represents a major blow to Suchard. In order to satisfy its aspirations to global leadership in the confectionery industry, it may seek to acquire Cadbury, which itself is vulnerable to a hostile bid. An agreed merger may prove mutually desirable. Suchard's options are so restricted because the two major US players are bid-proof – Mars is a private company and Hershey is controlled by a charitable trust (*Financial Times*, 24 June 1988).

ISSUES AND LESSONS

Well-managed and relatively successful companies are now subject to the attentions of takeover predators just as much as those companies where there is a clear failure of management and justification for change, though not necessarily of ownership. While there was scope for some improvement in Rowntree's performance in Europe, the fact is that the value of its brands was seen to be a critical element in the global expansion plans of Nestlé and Jacobs Suchard. This was so much so that Nestlé was prepared to pay a premium of 125 per cent over the share price prevailing before the battle, to secure victory.

It has been suggested by Rowntree management that the stock market had undervalued the company's brands and that this was to a large extent responsible for the bid. It may be that some of the blame in this regard could be laid at Rowntree's door in that brand performance and prospects could be expected to be reflected in share prices but only to the extent that full information is made available to the stock market. In this context, balance sheet valuations of brands are not necessarily the answer though estimates would no doubt be feasible. However, such an approach is alien to conventional accounting practice, which is limited to disclosing the historical cost of assets purchased rather than those developed internally. What is likely to be much more important is the full disclosure of brand sales and profit margins in the geographical markets served, as a basis for economic valuation by expert participants in the stock market. At the same time, it seems highly probable that the price paid for the brands was more a function of their value to Nestlé in the context of the firm's own global strategy. Thus the stock market's assessment of the value of the brands prior to the Nestlé bid would have been limited to Rowntree's situation and the business environment at that time.

In any event, Rowntree management, shareholders and employees would seem to have benefited financially from the Nestlé takeover, at least in the short term. The lack of 'reciprocity', which was used as an argument to defend Rowntree and was taken up strongly by John Banham, the Director General of the CBI, clearly has its price. If British companies are voluntarily to protect themselves from hostile bids as the Swiss do, through their shareholding arrangements, then shareholders must be prepared to accept a lower value for their shares or pursue other means to secure improved performance and prospects from company management.

The failure of Lord Young to refer the Swiss bids to the MMC was not surprising given the Government's general unwillingness to interfere in the 'public interest', except on competition grounds. On the basis of competitive effects in the UK market this was a correct decision. But it provides a classic example of the problem that current merger policy creates for the international competitiveness of UK companies. Given the prospect of a single European market by 1992 and the trend towards a globalization of markets, the focus on UK competition is unrealistically restrictive. In the EC context, a Swiss company, based outside the EC, could buy a British company and benefit from selling in the European market but a British company wanting to grow by acquisition to compete more effectively in Europe would be blocked by UK merger policy if its market share in Britain was 25 per cent or more. This has no doubt deterred many potential mergers which may have led to the development of UK-based international champions, e.g. a Cadbury Schweppes and Rowntree merger. In the 'bar wars', a Cadbury–Rowntree grouping would have been a global player. But now Cadbury itself is under threat from foreign predators, perhaps unnecessarily so.

TIMETABLE OF EVENTS

Nestlé vs Jacobs Suchard for Rowntree

1988

13 April:
Jacobs Suchard pays 629p (£162 m) to acquire a 14.9 per cent stake in Rowntree, whose shares stood at 477p the previous day. Suchard rules out a takeover bid for at least 1 year, unless a full bid elsewhere is lodged.

Rowntree shares close at 623p, valuing the York-based company at £1.3 bn.

26 April:
Nestlé launches £2.1 bn takeover bid for Rowntree.

27 April:
Conservative and Labour MPs begin a lobbying campaign to have Nestlé's offer referred to the Monopolies and Mergers Commission. Rowntree share price falls 2p to 926p due to the poor price received for the Tom's Foods disposal. The City had expected Rowntree to receive £150 m, but instead the price paid was only £107 m.

6 May:
It is disclosed that Rowntree is considering shedding jobs to rationalize its facilities in the UK and the Continent, in order to achieve a cost reduction of £20 m per year. Rowntree hopes to achieve single-source production by 1992.

9 May:
Tony Blair, Labour's Trade Spokesman, describes the Nestlé bid as 'a critical test of the Government's whole commitment to UK industry'.

10 May:
Speaking in the House of Commons, Kenneth Clarke, Industry Minister, indicates the likelihood of a non-referral of the Nestlé bid. Rowntree shares rise 2p to close at 905p.

11 May:
Debate continues in the House of Commons. Suchard sends letter to Rowntree requesting a meeting to discuss merger. Rowntree rejects this request.

12 May:
Sir Giles Shaw, former Industry Minister, tables a motion urging a review of merger policy which would highlight the issues of reciprocity.

23 May:
Lord Young receives Sir Gordon Borrie's recommendation that there are no grounds for referring either Nestlé's £2.1 bn bid or Jacobs Suchard's 29.9 per cent stake to the MMC.

Rowntree shares fall 2p to close at 892p.

24 May:
Lord Young, in interview with local radio station in Newcastle, says that 'if a foreign company were to buy Rowntree, I cannot feel that jobs are in jeopardy'. Rowntree shares rise 25p to close at 917p.

25 May:	Lord Young announces decision that both Nestlé and Suchard can proceed to bid for Rowntree. The Union Bank of Switzerland clears Suchard to make an offer of 940p provided the Rowntree board recommends the takeover bid.
	Rowntree shares close at £10, more than double their value of 13 April, when Suchard paid 629p per share.
26 May:	Rowntree issues defence document, in which it concentrates on stressing the value of its brands. Significantly, it is neither critical of Nestlé, nor does it argue for an independent Rowntree. The defence document also contains a profit forecast of £135 m in 1988, which exceeds the City's expectations.
	Suchard bids 950p for Rowntree, valuing the company at £2.3 bn. Rowntree shares close at £10.25.
27 May:	Rowntree shares close at £10.50, as rumours spread that Rowntree has recruited Goldman Sachs to find a 'white knight.'
1 June:	The General Municipal Boilermakers Union, the largest union representing Rowntree's 13,000 workforce, urges Rowntree board to recommend acceptance of the offer.
7 June:	Lord Young tells House of Lords at Question Time: 'I have no plans to introduce measures to inhibit foreign enterprises from investing in the UK by whatever means.' Nestlé allows the first closing date for its £2.1 bn bid to pass.
8 June:	The Government secures a comfortable majority of 98 (301–203) at the end of a half-day debate on its decision not to refer the Nestlé bid for Rowntree. Shadow Trade Spokesman, Bryan Gould, accuses the Government of 'dereliction of duty'.
13 June:	Suchard says it would invite Rowntree representatives to join its board, if it won the takeover battle. Its offer document also stresses that global management of Rowntree brands would continue to be conducted in York.
23 June:	Nestlè bids £2.622 billion (1075p per share) for Rowntree. Rowntree board recommends acceptance.

PART III

TAKEOVERS: RETROSPECT AND PROSPECT

12

Lesions and Lessons

This chapter attempts to highlight some of the main points that have emerged in the course of this book and to reflect on the lessons learned. It examines the prospects for takeovers and also looks at merger policy in an increasingly international business environment.

TAKEOVER COSTS AND BENEFITS

Opinion varies as to whether the current wave of mega-mergers has been beneficial for British industry and the national economy. Indeed it may be questioned whether such activity is beneficial for any national economy. On the one hand, it may be argued that the billions of pounds which companies have spent on takeover bids, whether as attacker or defender, have diverted funds from more urgent projects. Merchant banks and other advisers could be said to have encouraged the takeover trend and promoted the practice of hostile bids. Instead of investing that money in new technology, research and development, and staff training with an eye to the future, companies have tended to concentrate on the optimization of short-term performance rather than the long-term strategic investment and planning which British industry desperately needs.

Britain's largest trade union, the Transport and General Workers' Union, is disturbed by what it terms 'the casino atmosphere which currently prevails in the field of takeovers and mergers' (TGWU, 1986). It has been critical of the lack of precision in current merger policy, which 'leads to uncertainty and insecurity for companies and the workers they employ'. It has identified three main areas of concern which arise from the takeover flurry: job security, pension rights, and lack of employee disclosure and consultation (TGWU, 1986).

The financial institutions could also be criticized for their lack of a proactive approach to their investments, which could lead to beneficial changes in corporate strategy and management rather than a passive acceptance of the bonanza of a takeover deal.

On the other hand, the very threat of a bid has been sufficient to inject a new lease of life, though sometimes too late, into slumbering giants. In the course of recent mega-bids, Hanson Trust's Lord Hanson, Argyll's James Gulliver, BTR's Sir Owen Green and Elders' John Elliot may have ruffled a few feathers among the directors of Britain's blue chip companies and the City of London. This, some would argue, has been a small price to pay either for jolting the management of the target company into action, or having it replaced by more effective leadership. Moreover, the owners of the companies involved have benefited financially from the higher share prices which have resulted from such activity. However, whether or not the same result could have been achieved via a different route remains an open question.

TAKEOVER TACTICS

Apart from arguing the merits of takeovers as such, the tactics involved are also an issue of contention. Among the new takeover tactics that have emerged in the UK has been the leveraged bid, commonplace in the USA, by which the bidder finances the takeover by heavy borrowing secured on the assets of its target. Repayment is made from the not inconsiderable profits derived from selling off divisions or business units of the acquisition. In other words, the takeover is an asset-stripping operation. When the Australian conglomerate, Elders IXL, introduced the leveraged bid strategy to Britain in its audacious £1.8 bn offer for Allied-Lyons, it found itself referred to the Monopolies and Mergers Commission (MMC) for a review of its novel purchasing methods.

In addition to campaigning for a referral to the MMC, target firms too have pioneered new tactics. For example, Distillers, in its desperation to prevent an Argyll takeover, agreed to pay the costs incurred by its 'white knight' Guinness. Argyll viewed this arrangement as tantamount to a 'poison pill', because had it gained control of Distillers, it would have had to pay not just its own and Distillers' costs, but those of Guinness too. Since Distillers and Guinness concocted this arrangement, the Takeover Panel has ruled to prevent a similar deal happening again.

THE CREDIBILITY OF CITY REGULATION

Another outcome of the giant takeover battles that have recently taken place is the threat to the City of London's financial stability and credibility. This has arisen from the actions of some corporate predators and their advisers, often supposedly leading figures in the City's self-regulatory system, who have abandoned or bent the rules of financial orthodoxy in ruthless attempts to win control in contested bids. In their determination to win, some players have ridden roughshod over the Takeover Panel and have even, on occasion, shown similar disregard for the law. Action has been taken and extreme vigilance is now required to ensure that the potential for such scandalous behaviour is extremely restricted and, where it exists, severely penalized.

One of the lessons from the Guinness case worthy of further consideration concerns promises or undertakings made to the shareholders of the target company in takeover offer documents. There is a strong case for the directors of the bidding company to be held more accountable for their actions in such situations similar to the case in respect of prospectuses. There is also a strong case for more in-depth information to be given to investors, which will help them to make better judgements of the corporate strategy underlying mergers and the prospects of enhanced efficiency through synergy and other factors. More information about the impact of a merger on the job prospects of the workforces involved and on contracts with suppliers could also be encouraged together with some consideration of regional implications. In general terms, the more information companies are able to disclose, within competitive limits, the better it will be from the viewpoint of establishing a 'correct' or fair valuation for a company's shares, which is all-important in defending a takeover bid or in obtaining an acceptable price for a change of ownership.

As regards accounting and disclosure standards, a radical review of existing regulation is long overdue. If concerns about 'creative' accounting are to be resolved, then measures which reduce both uncertainty and the incentives for manipulation need to be introduced. The adoption of a single unified method of accounting for business combinations would seem desirable based on a modified and more restrictive form of 'acquisition' accounting, together with a substantial increase in the level of information disclosure.

The question of whether the City institutions of self-regulation, i.e. the Stock Exchange, the Takeover Panel and the Accounting Standards Committee, should be subject to more statutory control remains open and is subject to satisfactory performance in dealing with takeovers in the future.

THE IMPACT OF MERGER CONTROL

In every single mega-merger battle examined in this book the possibility of a referral to the MMC has loomed large. Indeed, in the seven takeover battles, four bidding firms had their bids referred to the MMC. Three of these were referred on competition grounds, but the Elders IXL bid for Allied-Lyons was referred because it was such a highly leveraged bid. The MMC cleared this bid, but Elders decided not to pursue Allied-Lyons, having acquired another brewer. The MMC blocked only one proposed merger, GEC's bid for Plessey, because it was concerned that the merger's anti-competitive effects would not be in the public interest. As was seen, two agreed mergers, Imperial's bid for United Biscuits and Guinness's bid for Distillers, were also referred. By referring these bids, the regulatory authorities had virtually assured victory for the hostile bidders, Hanson and Argyll, which had bid for Imperial and Distillers respectively. However, United Biscuits and Guinness, both of which were advised by Morgan Grenfell, took unprecedented steps to overcome the regulatory hurdle. First of all, United Biscuits, which was originally the target company, switched places and bid for Imperial. At the same time, it had discussions with the Office of Fair Trading in order to identify what action was necessary to avoid a referral to the MMC. The solution was to divest the snack foods division of Imperial. Guinness took plea bargaining a stage further and persuaded the MMC that it had abandoned its original bid. The MMC thus allowed Guinness to mount a reformulated bid which included the divestment of five whisky brands. By the time Dixons bid for Woolworth, it was apparent that a referral to the MMC could be avoided by assuring the OFT that certain divestments would be undertaken. Dixons thus promised to divest Comet and the OFT allowed its bid to proceed.

Competition was not an issue in BTR's bid for Pilkington. Nevertheless, there was an intensive campaign to have the bid referred because of the alleged differences in corporate culture, plus the possible impact on employment and the transfer of control from the North-West to London. The Government claims that UK merger policy is not based exclusively on competition, but the decision not to refer this case to the MMC suggests that UK merger policy is in fact based almost entirely on competition grounds. Bids will not be referred because of the possible effects on a regional economy, nor because of the effect on employment. Apart from competition grounds, a proposed merger may be referred if the bid is highly leveraged. In the case of the Nestlé and Suchard bids for Rowntree, the 'reciprocity' argument was not accepted as the basis for a referral and there were no competition grounds given the focus of merger policy on the effect of a merger on the UK domestic market.

INTERNATIONAL TAKEOVERS: TRENDS AND IMPLICATIONS

Since the mid-1980s, there has been a dramatic increase in large international takeovers. These deals have been due to the determination of companies to add best-selling brands to existing portfolios, or simply to gain market share to improve their ranking in their core businesses. UK companies have spent heavily on US acquisitions with a boom in deals worth $100 m or more.

UK companies such as Beazer, Blue Arrow, Grand Metropolitan, Hanson, ICI, Ladbroke and Tate & Lyle have all made a US acquisition worth more than $1 bn, not to mention Shell and Unilever, the Anglo-Dutch giants. Furthermore, famous brand names such as Hilton, Jacuzzi, Smith & Wesson, Smirnoff, Vaseline, to name but a few, have fallen into UK hands.

While UK companies have been the greatest spenders, companies from other European countries, and from Japan, have also made major acquisitions in the USA. For example, companies which have broken the billion-dollar barrier include BASF and Hoechst of Germany, Elf Aquitaine and Thomson of France, and Bridgestone and Sony of Japan. In 1988, Switzerland's Hoffman-La Roche became the first foreign company to bid more than $4.0 bn for a non-oil US company. La Roche was eventually outbid by Kodak which paid in excess of $5.0 bn to gain Sterling Drug. The defeat of La Roche means that the largest ever US takeover by a Swiss company remains Nestlé's $3.0 bn purchase of Carnation in 1985.

This brief review of US takeovers by foreign companies is enough to underline America's 'open door' policy to foreign investors, even if that includes the acquisition of US assets rather than simply greenfield investment. Like the USA, Britain has adopted a similar policy to foreign investors. Hence, foreign companies are as free as any domestic company to acquire any UK company. In most other European countries, however, it is almost impossible to acquire companies unless the incumbent management welcomes the takeover bid. Hostile takeover bids stand to fail for a variety of reasons. In West Germany, the large banks have sizeable stakes in the corporate sector and they can use their influence to remove unsuccessful management, rather than rely on a takeover to achieve the same effect – there is perhaps a lesson here for

British financial institutions. In Switzerland, the shareholding system and distinction between voting and non-voting shares are enough to render most companies bid-proof. In early 1988, for example, two Swiss chemical giants, Ciba-Geigy and Sandoz, restructured their shareholdings to erect an even stronger defence against a hostile bidder.

Clearly then, UK companies are much more likely to be acquired in a hostile takeover bid situation than their Continental European counterparts. This distinction has come to the fore because of the two hostile bids by Swiss companies for Rowntree, Britain's second largest confectioner. The UK Government has decided that it will adhere rigidly to its policy of referring bids on competition grounds only. This is being applied even in those cases where foreign bidders are bid-proof. Admittedly, a distinction has to be made between companies that are bid-proof because of shareholding arrangements, and those that are safe from foreign bidders because of legislation, such as the Foreign Takeovers Act in Australia. In the case of Swiss companies, the former is the case. Since UK companies can, if they wish, avail themselves of a similar defence mechanism, they can have little cause for complaint when they receive a hostile bid from a company whose shareholders agree to such a defence. By so doing, Swiss shareholders sacrifice the possibility of a huge increase in the share price of their company which normally occurs when a firm becomes a target, as the Rowntree case illustrates. In order to maintain control in Britain of UK companies, institutional investors and the companies themselves must decide whether to install Swiss-type defences.

The alternative means of thwarting foreign takeovers is through political intervention, but the Nestlé case suggests that such a prospect is unlikely. Consequently, speculation has increased that many more top UK companies with best-selling brands could be acquired. Since Nestlé won Rowntree, four further billion pound-plus bids involving foreign companies have been launched. In July 1988, Australia's Goodman Fielder Wattie offered £1.7 bn for Ranks Hovis McDougall, the food and flour group, whose brands include Bisto, Mr Kipling Cakes, Mother's Pride and Robertson's Jams. However, this bid was subsequently withdrawn following referral to the MMC. In September 1988, a record bid of £2.9 bn was made by the South African-controlled Minorco group for Consolidated Gold Fields. This was followed in October by Elders IXL's £1.6 bn bid for Scottish and Newcastle. Both these bids have been referred to the MMC.

In the light of recent events, it is possible that the Government may be forced to rethink its 'open door' policy. While the free market approach may be desirable in principle there is a case for ensuring some sovereignty, or independence, of decision-making at the UK corporate level as well as at the parliamentary level. Foreign direct investment may be a sought after prize (witness the response when Ford decided not to locate its electronics plant in the UK), but multinational corporations (MNCs), even those with decentralized structures, tend to centre activities with the greatest added value in the home country, rather than the host nation. It is clearly important, therefore, to the UK economy that Britain continues as a major home nation to large MNCs, rather than be merely a popular location for foreign investors.

Further, having an 'open door' policy is fine so long as the USA, the most popular destination for outward UK investment, shares this policy too. Should the USA adopt a tougher line on foreign investment, then the UK would be foolish not to do likewise. Already, there are signs of political opposition to foreign 'invaders' in the USA. Similarly, in the EC context it would seem important that the UK does not offer any unnecessary advantages to hostile bidders relative to its European partners.

Finally, should companies such as Allied-Lyons, Beechams, Cadbury Schweppes, Fisons, Pearson, Ranks Hovis McDougall, Scottish and Newcastle and United Biscuits be acquired by foreign interests, then the UK Government will face enormous pressure to curb foreign expansion in the UK. Despite the Conservative majority such pressure can be effective, as Margaret Thatcher discovered when she mooted plans to sell Austin Rover to Ford. Eventually, a 'British solution' was found, with British Aerospace buying the business.

As a result of the above trends, it is predicted that there will eventually be a dramatic shift in government policy in respect of the foreign acquisition of UK companies. Positive measures are needed now to encourage companies to become stronger and better able to defend themselves against unwanted and unnecessary foreign predators. The danger is that this may not occur until the mid-1990s, by which time only the 'second XI' will be left.

EC MERGER POLICY

The prospect of a single European market by 1992 has concentrated political minds to consider the question of merger policy covering competition in the European market as a whole, rather than just each of the national markets as at present. A variety of national policies becomes increasingly redundant as the volume of international takeovers, and especially cross-border European mergers, increases as outlined above.

Peter Sutherland, the former EC Competition Commissioner from Ireland, aimed to establish EC controls on all major community-wide acquisitions and mergers. At present the EC Commission has the right to intervene in mergers on competition grounds only *after* the event. The new proposals would establish a framework for clarifying in advance whether a merger is considered desirable.

The EC's 1973 draft Regulation on merger control has now been revived (Commission of the European Communities, 1988). This would cover mergers in which the combined annual sales of the parties involved was ECU 1 bn (approx. $1.2 bn) with each company having sales greater than ECU 100 m. Rather than setting percentage limits for EC market share, the EC Commission would study each merger case by case on a pragmatic basis. However, a European market share of 25 per cent or less would be deemed compatible with EC competition policy. The regulations would cover transnational mergers, where both parties are in different member states, where one of them has major subsidiaries throughout the Community, or even when a group based outside the EC acquires a company with a presence in several member states. Under the draft Regulation, the Commission would have one month to decide on whether to be involved and then up to five months to rule on whether a proposed merger restricts competition. Companies would have to file detailed information about a proposed acquisition, including its potential effect on competition, employment, research and development, and market share. In addition, proposals concerning the disclosure of shareholdings in target companies are likely to be introduced.

Opponents of the EC proposal are opposed to a further layer of bureaucracy on top of national merger legislation (though not all member states have merger controls). They have also expressed concern that if the Commission was slow to deliver a verdict, the target company may rush into the arms of a non-EC 'white knight'.

The Commission argues, paradoxically as Peter Sutherland himself has conceded, that in competition policy, more control means more freedom. The latest, the 17th, report on competition policy points to a significant increase in cross-border mergers in the Community. The number of large (i.e. sales of more than ECU 1 bn) mergers at national and cross-border level also increased from 227 in 1986 to 303 in 1987 (Commission of the European Communities, 1988). This growth suggests an urgent need for community-wide legislation which would harmonize national merger controls. As Peter Sutherland, the EC Commissioner, has said, 'It's totally unreal to have separate merger control regulations being adopted and applied by different member states, which could lead to different conclusions about the same community-scale merger ... The fact of international competition, the fact that there are other producers from other parts of the world who have access to the market would be considered in deciding whether or not a merger creates difficulty for us' (*The Wall Street Journal*, 24 March 1988).

The response of the French and UK Governments to the EC proposals is still somewhat non-commital though it seems that there is now EC-wide agreement on the general principle that the European Commission should have the final say on potentially anti-competitive international takeovers. From a UK perspective, however, more emphasis on the European market dimension would tend to unshackle British companies from a currently restrictive UK merger policy focused on domestic market competition. At the same time, it would enable an entirely new aspect to be considered which is currently not taken into account by the UK authorities, namely the effect of a UK takeover by a foreign company on competition in the rest of Europe. It may be that a merger which has negligible effects on competition in the UK has a detrimental effect on competition in Europe. The Nestlé takeover of Rowntree, for example, may have significantly reduced competition in Europe because by eliminating Rowntree as an actual or potential competitor in Continental European markets, it may have enhanced its market power to an unacceptable level. Issues of EC competition can only be resolved at a community-wide level, thus underlining the necessity for an effective and acceptable system of EC merger controls to be established sooner rather than later. In doing so, it would also seem important to ensure that national regulations are co-ordinated and that the playing field is as level as possible across the Community.

UK MERGER POLICY AND INTERNATIONAL COMPETITION: THE WAY FORWARD?

Given the dual concerns with preserving competition in the domestic market and with the international competitiveness of British companies, the policy-makers must strive to strike the correct balance between the two. It has been argued by some that both objectives are perfectly compatible, but others are of the view that these are conflicting objectives and that existing merger policy is detrimental so far as international competitiveness is concerned.

It is to be hoped that the Government may seek, or be compelled, to resolve this tension between domestic and international competition by adopting a more flexible approach. Paradoxically, by concentrating attention on domestic competition, UK policy-makers in effect have interfered with market forces to the detriment of British business. Conglomerates have been encouraged at the expense of companies wishing to develop strong core businesses with international muscle. As the President of the CBI, Sir Trevor Holdsworth, said in a recent speech: 'We need a competition policy which does not frustrate Britain's need for the creation of more internationally competitive, very large, product and market-oriented companies comparable to the giants of the US and Japan' (*Financial Times*, 9 June 1988).

CONCLUDING REMARKS

The mega-merger mayhem experienced in recent takeover battles may have had a positive effect in terms of the clarification and development of UK merger policy, but some weaknesses have also been revealed, notably in respect of the unwillingness to recognize fully the implications of the growing globalization of markets and the impact of the 1992 single European market. Mega-merger battles have also underlined some deficiencies in the regulations relating to corporate conduct and accountability administered by self-regulatory organizations such as the Takeover Panel, the Stock Exchange and the Accounting Standards Committee. While some reforms have been prompted by events, there is scope for further improvement and continued vigilance. The challenge now is to refine merger policy and make the system of controls relating both to competition and corporate conduct more effective, and in a way that is also more sensitive to the reality of international competition and economic integration in both the European Community and global business environment.

References and Further Reading

Accounting Principles Board (1970a) Opinion no. 16, *Business Combinations*, AICPA, New York.

Accounting Principles Board (1970b) Opinion no. 17, *Intangible Assets*, AICPA, New York.

Acquisitions Monthly, Annual Review of 1986, 1987; Half-yearly Review, 1988.

Begg, P. F. C. (1986) *Corporate Acquisitions and Mergers*, Graham & Trotman.

Boesky, Ivan F. (1985) *Merger Mania*, Bodley Head.

Borrie, G. (1986a) Speech to the Finance Houses Association, 2 April 1986.

Borrie, G. (1986b) Speech to the Glasgow Discussion Group on Finance and Investment, 4 December 1986.

Borrie, G. (1987a) Stockton Lectures: European Competitiveness, Deregulation and Competition at Home as Prerequisites for Success Abroad, 15 January 1987.

Borrie, G. (1987b) Speech to the Conference on Takeovers and Mergers, University of Glasgow, 21 May 1987.

Buckley, P. J. and Casson, M. (1976) *The Future of the Multinational Enterprise*, Macmillan.

Business Monitor, MQ7, *Acquisitions and Mergers of Industrial and Commercial Companies*, HMSO.

Buxton, N. (1986) *Performance and Problems of Scotland's Industry and the Economy*, Scottish Council for Development and Industry. Edinburgh.

Chikoti, S. B. (1987) BTR–Pilkington: a case study. Project for Master of Accountancy degree, University of Glasgow.

Chiplin, B. and Wright, M. (1987) *The Logic of Mergers*, Hobart Paper no. 107, Institute of Economic Affairs, London.

Clark, J. J. (1985) *Business Merger and Acquisition Strategies*, Prentice-Hall.

Commission of the European Communities (1983) *Seventh Council Directive on Consolidated Accounts*, Brussels.

Commission of the European Communities (1988) *17th Report on Competition Policy*, Brussels.

Companies Act 1985, HMSO, London.

Confederation of British Industry (1987) *Merger and Acquisition Accounting*, Consultation paper, July.

Cooke, T. (1986) *Mergers and Acquisitions*. Basil Blackwell.

Cooke, T. (1988) *International Mergers and Acquisitions*, Basil Blackwell.

Davidson, Kenneth M. (1985) *Mega-Mergers. Corporate America's Billion-Dollar Takeovers*, Ballinger Publishing Company.

Department of Trade and Industry (1988a) *DTI – the Department for Enterprise*, HMSO, London, January.

Department of Trade and Industry (1988b) *Mergers Policy*, HMSO, London.

Dicken, Peter (1986) *Global Shift. Industrial Change in a Turbulent World*, Harper & Row.

Dunn, J. (1987) Dixons–Woolworth: a case study. Project for Master of Accountancy degree, University of Glasgow.

Dunning, J. H. (1980) Towards an eclectic theory of international production, *Journal of International Business Studies*, Spring/Summer.

Dunning, J. H. (1981) *International Production and the Multinational Enterprise*, Allen & Unwin.

Dunning, J. H. (1988) The eclectic paradigm of international production: a restatement and some possible extensions, *Journal of International Business Studies*, Spring.

Fallon, Ivan and Srodes, James (1987) *Takeovers*, Hamish Hamilton.

The Financial Services Act 1986, HMSO.

Firth, M. (1976) *Share Prices and Mergers*, Gower.

Firth, M. (1980) Takeovers, shareholder returns and the theory of the firm, *Quarterly Journal of Economics*, no. 94.

Franko, L. (1976) *The European Multinationals*, Harper & Row.

Franks, J. and Harris, R. (1986) *Shareholder Wealth Effects of Corporate Takeovers: The UK Experience 1955–85*, Working Paper, London Business School.

Goldberg, W. H. (1983) *Mergers – Motives, Modes, Methods*, Gower.

Gray, S. J. (1988) Accounting for acquisitions and mergers: a unified approach, *The Accountant's Magazine*, July.

Gray, S. J. and McDermott, M. C. (1988) International mergers and takeovers: a review of trends and recent developments, *European Management Journal*, Spring.

Gray, S. J., Campbell, L. G. and Shaw, J. C. (1984) *International Financial Reporting*, Macmillan.

Griffiths, Ian (1986) *Creative Accounting*, Sidgwick & Jackson.

Holl, P. and Pickering, J. F. (1986) *The Determinants and Effects of Actual, Abandoned and Contested Mergers*, UMIST.

Hopt, K. J. (ed.) (1982) *European Merger Control*, Walter de Gruyter.

Hymer, S. H. (1976) *The International Operations of National Firms*, Lexington Books.

Iacocca, L. (1988) *Talking Straight*, Sidgwick & Jackson.

Institute of Chartered Accountants in England and Wales (1984) SSAP no. 22 *Accounting for Goodwill*.

Institute of Chartered Accountants in England and Wales (1985) SSAP no. 23 *Accounting for Acquisitions and Mergers.*

Institute of Chartered Accountants in England and Wales (1987) *Financial Reporting 1986–87. A Survey of UK Published Accounts*, ICAEW.

Jensen, M. C. and Ruback, R. S. (1983) The market for corporate control: the scientific evidence, *Journal of Financial Economics*, April, vol. 11, nos. 1–4.

Keenan, M. and White, L. J. (1982) *Mergers and Acquisitions*, Lexington Books.

Khoury, Sarkis (1980) *Transnational Mergers and Acquisitions in the United States*, Lexington Books.

Kochan, N. and Pym, H. (1987) *The Guinness Affair*, Christopher Helm.

Leigh-Pemberton, R. (1987) A speech to Overseas Bankers Club, 2 February 1987.

McDermott, M. C. (1989) *Multinationals: Foreign Divestment and Disclosure*, McGraw-Hill.

McDermott, M. C. and Gray, S. J. (1988) International brands in international takeovers: the fatal attraction, *Acquisitions Monthly*, August.

McPhail, F. (1987) The Distillers Company Limited: Anatomy of a Takeover, BAcc (Hons) Dissertation, University of Glasgow.

Meeks, G. (1977) *Disappointing Marriage: A Study of the Gains from Mergers*, Cambridge University Press.

Michel, Allen and Shaked, Israel (1986) *Takeover Madness. Corporate America Fights Back*, Wiley.

Moir, C. (1986) *The Acquisitive Streak: An Analysis of the Takeover and Merger Boom*, Hutchinson Business.

Monopolies and Mergers Commission (1986) *The General Electric Company PLC and The Plessey Company PLC: A Report on the Proposed Merger*, HMSO Cmnd 9867.

Mueller, D. (ed.) (1980) *The Determinants and Effects of Mergers – An International Comparison*, Gunn and Ham.

Office of Fair Trading (1985a, 1986, 1987) *Annual Report of the Director General of Fair Trading*, HMSO.

Office of Fair Trading (1985b) *Mergers: A Guide to the Procedures under the Fair Trading Act 1973*, HMSO.

Organization for Economic Co-operation and Development, *Annual Reports on Competition Policy in OECD Member Countries*, OECD, Paris.

Organization for Economic Co-operation and Development (1974) *Mergers and Competition Policy*, OECD, Paris.

Organization for Economic Co-operation and Development (1984) *Merger Policies and Recent Trends in Mergers*, OECD, Paris.

Organization for Economic Co-operation and Development, Committee on Competition Law and Policy (1988) *International Mergers and Competition Policy*, OECD, Paris.

Panel on Takeovers and Mergers (1988a) *The City Code on Takeovers and Mergers and the Rules Governing Substantial Acquisitions of Shares* (rev. ed.).

Panel on Takeovers and Mergers (1988b) *The Takeover Panel: Report on the Year ended 31st March 1988.*

Porter, M. (1980) *Competitive Strategy*, Free Press.

Porter, M. (1985) *Competitive Advantage*, Free Press.

Porter, M. (ed.) (1986) *Competition in Global Industries*, Harvard Business School Press.

Porter, M. (1987) From competitive advantage to corporate strategy, *Harvard Business Review*, May–June.

Prais, S. J. (1981) *The Evolution of Giant Firms in Britain*, Cambridge University Press.

Pugh, P. (1987) *Is Guinness Good for You?: Bid for Distillers – The Inside Story*, Blackstone Press.

Rugman, A. M., Lecraw, D. J. and Booth, L. D. (1985) *International Business: Firm and Environment*, McGraw-Hill.

Scottish Council for Development and Industry (1986) Memorandum to the Department of Trade and Industry, *Review of Law and Policy on Mergers and Restrictive Trade Practices*, 22 August.

Shapiro, A. (1986) *Multinational Financial Management*, Allyn and Bacon.

Singh, A. (1971) *Take-Overs: Their Relevance to the Stock Market and Theory of the Firm*, Cambridge University Press.

Stern, J. M. and Chew, D. H. (eds) (1986) *The Revolution in Corporate Finance*, Basil Blackwell.

Taylor, P. A. (1987) *Consolidated Financial Statements*, Paul Chapman Publishing.

Taylor, Peter and Turley, Stuart (1986) *The Regulation of Accounting*, Basil Blackwell.

Transport and General Workers' Union (1986) *TGWU Submission to the MMC Regarding the Proposed Takeover of Allied-Lyons PLC by Elders IXL*, London.

Utton, M. A. (1982) *The Political Economy of Big Business*, Martin Robertson.

Walker, David (1987) Speech to the Conference on Takeovers and Mergers, University of Glasgow, 21 May 1987.

Index